MW00850180

MY LIFE AS A CHILD ACTOR: Chaos, Cruelty, & Laughter

MY LIFE AS A CHILD ACTOR

Chaos, Cruelty, & Laughter

The story of Rory Shevin

Written by Rory Shevin

AKA Rory Stevens

ISBN: 978 0 578 33 756 2

DEDICATION

Dear Beth,

I am dedicating this story book to you for without your continued encouragement this story would never have seen the light of day. It would have stayed buried in a place that I have never been willing to go until now. For this and so much more, I am beyond grateful to both you and all our amazing children and grandchildren – both biological and adopted. I want to express my unending love and admiration for my siblings – without your strength, support and love I simply would not be here today. I am so appreciative for all my wonderful nieces, nephews and their children, as well. Thank you all for helping to change my view of what family meant and filling my life with compassion, excitement, joy and love. Beth, you showed me how not to become that lonely old man sitting by myself while life passed me by.

All my love,

-Rory

CONTENTS

CAST OF "CHARACTERS"

Grandpa Julius	"Here lay the family jewels"
Grandma Rose	"But, the cookies were for you"
Fred Shevin (Dad)	"She has many nice qualities"
Elaine Shevin (Mom)	"The food was mine, for Mom only, not yours, don't touch, hands off"
Randie (Big sister)	"The saddest day of my life"
Marc (Big brother)	"I will never let you hit one of us again"
Rory (Me)	"RED ALERT" -or- "DON'T CALL THE FIRE DEPARTMENT"
Stacey (Little sister)	"Stop poking me"
Sugar (The dog)	run, run, run
Eric (The cat)	Yuk - gross
The House	1938 special

Prologue – The Birds

Filmed in 1963

Child Actor – Rory Stevens

9 years old

Available on Amazon Prime

When I was nine years old I worked as a child actor with famed movie director Alfred Hitchcock on his horror classic, The Birds. Even though I had only one line of dialogue in the entire picture, I was on set for three weeks for filming. At one point Alfred Hitchcock felt the need to take me aside to explain the next scene, the scene with the birds. He was worried that I was going to be frightened by all the birds flying around. He took me aside, "you will see dozens of birds flying around" the famed director explained, "but only eight birds have been trained to fly in and appear as if they are attacking people. The other birds will just fly around. Now you understand about the other birds, don't you?" "Sure" I replied, "they are only extras!" This brought the house down with laughter, whistles, and shout-outs from all of the workers on the set – from the actors and extras, to the camera men, lighting & sound technicians, wardrobe & make-up people, not to mention the bird handlers, and so many more. It was quite an unexpected moment that lives on in infamy between a nine year old child actor and a world renowned director. As the movie built to a crescendo, just as the gas station was about to explode in what may be the movie's most memorable scene, I cried out, "Mommy are the birds going to eat us?" Just this… and I was on the set for three weeks for this movie that has lasted in infamy for nearly 50 years now and counting. To this day, 59 years later, I am still getting residuals that pay once every year or so (between $10.00 and $20.00) whenever this movie plays. I have no idea what I earned from working on this movie at the time, just as I had no idea what I earned from any of the acting I did as a child, as that was all controlled by my parents.

Valley's Child Star Shatters Poise Of Ace Director Alfred Hitchcock

When nine year old Valleyite Rory Stevens was working on the set of "The Birds," Director Alfred Hitchcock took him aside to explain the next scene to him.

"Of all these birds flying around," said the famed direchor, "only eight are trained to fly in and attack the people. Now you understand about the other birds, don't you?"

"Sure," replied Rory, "They are only extras!"

Only a child reared in show business would probably have given an answer like that and handsome and blonde Rory has been working steadily since his first job on "Playhouse 90" at the age of five and a half.

He has played starring parts in such shows as "Leave It To Beaver" and "Morning Court" and been featured in innumerable others such as "The Lloyd Bridges" Show, "Aloca Premiere," "Sam Benedict," "The Untouchables," "G. E. True," "Dr. Kildare," "Wagon Train," "Going My Way," "McKeever & The Colonel," "The Andy Griffith" Show and others.

In his private life Rory is

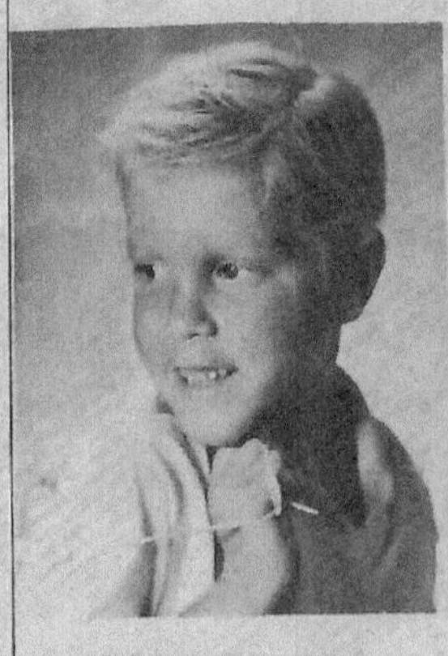

RORY STEVENS

enormously self-sufficient wa beyond his years. An A studen in all subjects, he is an amaz ing all around athlete for hi 50 inches who specializes i tennis and swimming.

Yet, show business has lef no mark on this soft spoke child who wins friends and in fluences people wherever h goes.

Rory's entire family is activ in show business. His ten an a half year old brother Marc just finished the juvenile lea in the stage play "Have I Gc A Girl For You" at the Bilt more and is now doing a "Kra TV Theater."

His twelve year old siste Randie, has chalked up a lon list of movie and TV credit including the current "Papa' Delicate Condition" and jus recently was chosen "Pillsbur Girl of the Year" and signed t do a series of commercials fo the company.

Introduction

The following is a true story of two adults who became parents and made an attempt to raise a family of four children. A story about parents who were quite poor, with little to nothing to their name. Each week, they could barely put together enough money to feed their growing (very athletic as it turns out) family. It is a story about how these four children found creative ways to stave off hunger – finding what they could eat on the floor, in the trash, or growing on the trees in the neighborhood around them. This is a story of parental abuse, where the kids were beaten (literally) black and blue simply for trying to find food to eat and to make their way in the world. This story is also about much more. It is about four kids that would not be put down or held back, no matter what. A story about four kids that became so close through their adversity that they hold a lifelong bond that, to this day, cannot be broken. This is a story about four kids who had little right to survive, let alone succeed, and all did so each in their own grand fashion.

>**Stacey** who would become a championship swimmer, obtain a law degree, happily marry a wonderful man, and become the mother of her own four children.

>**Marc** who happily married, fathered two beautiful young ladies of his own, and would come to change the face of Southern California residential real estate brokerage, setting records beyond what was thought possible.

>**Randie** who is also joyfully married, a mother to two grown (and quite successful) young men, who became a champion swimmer, and moved on to become a volleyball player on the U.S. National Women's Team, then studied hard to earn a EdD., is an accomplished author with multiple books under her belt, teacher and a lecturer who aims to make a real difference in this world we all live in.

>Lastly, it is a story about me, **Rory**, someone who has endured a lot and grew stronger because of it all. Someone who made a solemn vow not to raise children the way his parents did but to raise them in a home full of love where their dreams and goals were supported, not the other way around. Someone who worked for over 40 years in real estate as a partner with my brother, under the moniker "Marc and Rory Shevin." As of writing this book, I have been happily married for over 34 years;

I have two wonderful biological children, and two incredible adopted children who are all living happy, loving, and productive lives. I remain incredibly close with all of my siblings and all of our children are close cousins and friends with one another.

No matter how all of this began, thankfully we have all ended up in a very good place… but let's introduce the rest of the "cast" so you can get a better picture of how we ended up where we did.

Marc, Randie, Stacey, & Rory

Julius Gostel (Grandpa)

Let's begin with short back stories on our key characters. My story, and this story, actually begins with a young man named Julius Gostel, who would one day become my grandfather. He was born in Vienna, Austria and, like so many others, when he was around 14 years of age his parents sent him to America to find a better life. His is just one of the many stories you still hear of this migration. Without a single penny in his pocket, zero knowledge of the language, and younger than the 18 years required for entry into The United States at the time, he somehow made his way through Ellis Island to America. He was young and strong and found work fast. He used to tell us how he earned ten cents a day and that he saved a few pennies out of each dime he earned. He liked to tell stories of life in New York, after a hard day's work, the eateries would have big signs out front advertising a large mug of beer for five cents plus an all you can eat meal thrown in for free. This was how he was able to get on his feet and begin a real life in America.

Grandpa Jules

Julius was never out of work a single day in his life and he was very proud of that fact. He candled eggs on his sisters farm, worked on the railroad checking the tracks for safety issues, sold furniture in retail, was a German-speaking radio announcer for a furniture company, was a parking lot attendant, ran an import/export warehouse as a manager, was a taxi driver, and even bought an Orange Julius concession stand, which we had endless laughs poking fun at the similarity in their names. His last job before retiring was as a stock clerk in an art supply store.

He was our grandpa (my Mom's dad) and we called him Jules or just Grandpa. He was strong in spirit, self- taught, worked hard, and made a pretty good life for himself. He often worked two full time jobs, particularly during the depression-era. Grandpa Julius was loved and admired for his work. As he hit the mandatory retirement age, his boss pretended not to notice as neither he nor Grandpas' colleagues could bear to see him go. However, by the time Grandpa reached 90 years old, it became impossible to continue to hide his age. So with great fanfare, including a full page story in the local newspaper about him, he decided to retire and live out his days with his family in the San Francisco Bay area of California. He was glad to be alive and celebrated that fact every single day. We occasionally got to visit Grandpa where he and his family lived in the Bay Area, or Grandpa would come down south to Los Angeles, California to visit us.

After a few years had passed, and Grandpa was well into his late 90s, he tired of the Bay area and decided to come down south to live with Mom and us (the boys). Each morning, he would do a little dance in a circle and throw his hands into the air and exclaim "what a beautiful day it certainly was." We all treasured the time Grandpa spent with us, he was simply a joy to be around. However, when he passed away Mom surpassed her usual level of bonkers we had become accustomed to. She did not want the trouble of dealing with or having to pay the expenses for his funeral and burial. She simply put his body into a box, put the box onto a train, and "mailed" my grandfather's body to the rest of her family in San Francisco. She did this without calling ahead, as calling long distance at that time was very expensive, to let them know that Julius had passed away. Nor did she give them advance notice that she was shipping them his body. Nope, nothing at all. Mom's family in San Francisco simply received a notification that they had a large package to be picked up at the train station, no more than that. Of course, off they went to the train station to collect their package… and after opening it they received the shock of their lives. THEY NEVER SPOKE TO MOM AGAIN.

Marc and I (to put a small smile on this nightmare) came up with a epitaph we wanted to put on Grandpa's grave. **"Here Lies the Family Jewels**" (as Jules was his nickname) – and, at the time, we thought it was the funniest idea we had ever had.

Elaine (Mom), Rory, Stacey, Grandpa Julius

Rose Gostel (Grandma)

Rose was born in Lithuania on the Polish border. Her marriage to Julius was an arranged marriage, as her mother wanted her to go to America and marry into a more elegant family. Rose was sent to America to marry Julius when she was 17 years old and he was 21. They ended up settling in Manhattan where Rose had some other family living. Since they were a young couple they did not have any money and lived with Rose's family for a while; they even began their small family while living there. Unfortunately, they were never well suited for one other... or at least that was what we were told when we would ask why they did not live together. But I digress… Rose eventually found work in New Jersey, sewing in a dress factory, to help earn money during the depression while Julius got a second job driving a taxi cab. They ended up having two kids together, Elaine (my Mom) and her brother Stanley.

Rose wanted to raise Elaine as a proper "lady", according to what was acceptable at the time, and forced her into all of the appropriate feminine lessons – including piano lessons. All the while Elaine fought back and simply became more and more "un-lady like" the more her mother pushed. Rose said she was a tom boy and called her a "wild Indian" when she would do cartwheels or hang upside down on the bars in the playground while her panties showed as her skirt dropped over her face.

As you will come to read in the following chapters, a lot of our family stories revolve around food, even as far back as Rose and Julius' day. Rose told a lot of stories of being very poor and of having very little meat to eat for weeks and weeks. Oddly enough, she did have a pet chicken at one point when she was young. One night, even though they had no money to buy meat, the family all shared a decently delicious boiled chicken for dinner... with soup, potatoes, and bread. After dinner, when Rose went outside to play, she could not find her pet chicken to play with. When the realization finally hit her where the chicken for dinner had come from, she was so traumatized that she refused to eat chicken again for many years.

Elaine with Grandma Rose

Rose also lived with her cousin, Joe. His parents had passed away and he was brought in and raised with her and her brother by their parents. One evening, during dinner, she and Joe had a fight over a bowl of sour cream that was at the center of the table for dipping their hot boiled potato in. She accused him of getting more than his share. He got angry and shoved the side of his hand into the sour cream shouting, "this is my half and this is yours!" Fighting about food, as you will see, is also a running theme in this family.

When I was a kid, Cousin Joe visited us quite often. We had a family saying, "Good old Cousin Joe, he is moving kind of slow." I was about 16 years of age and just learning to drive when Joe, who was getting on in years, fell ill suddenly. He had no other family beside us and my family was already struggling to survive. Cousin Joe turned up on our doorstep and honestly seemed to be dying; there was really nothing we could do to help him. Nobody else wanted to deal with him or his illness problems, so I was forced to take Joe to the hospital and drop him off. We never saw Cousin Joe again after that day.

Grandma Rose with Randie

The one thing that Rose and Julius instilled in their children was:

"NEVER TO QUIT AND ALWAYS TO ACHIEVE"

Fred Shevin (Dad)

Fred was born in New York on May 8, 1916 into a family of nine children. As were the times, they grew up in a period of war and severe economic depression. As such, his family was scattered and not very close with one another (either in proximity or relationship), like Dad would have wished for. He dreamed of having his own family and a stable home with a lush garden and beautiful full fruit trees. Eventually, he did decide to move to California where he met Elaine, married, and started the family he had been dreaming of since he was a child.

Fred and Elaine

However, Mom and Dad were very poor and constantly fought over money to buy groceries, clothes for the kids to wear to school… or just about anything for that matter. Everything we received as kids was handed down. We never knew what it was like to buy something new from a store, go to a restaurant, or go on a vacation… that was simply unheard of!

Mom eventually got a job with the Parks & Recreation department with the city teaching tennis and swimming (I will elaborate on this later). Dad had trouble landing steady work due to being Jewish (as he would say to us). He did work for labor unions for a time but preferred writing and barely eked out a living writing advertising materials and trying to sell self-written screen plays. This was no doubt how he got the idea to put his children into show business. As each of the four of us came along, Mom and Dad would try to help us land any TV acting parts that they were able to with connections Dad had made through his work.

I was four years old when my parents decided I was going to become a successful child actor. Dad felt he might know who to talk to or who to see to help "jump start" my new career. He did not want anyone to think he was helping me along, so my parents decided to change my name from Rory Shevin to Rory Stevens, and that was to be my stage name forevermore. His connections actually panned out too. When my career as a child actor started to come together, you might think that would have been a good thing for my struggling family, unless you actually knew my parents – for this is really when it all started going downhill.

Elaine and Fred before kids

Dad continued his writing work at the dining room table on his Royal Typewriter and Rotary Phone with Mom in the adjoining kitchen. On a daily basis, Mom was there yelling at Dad about everything she could think of while he pecked away on his typewriter and took phone calls. I remember listening to Dad trying to make deals on the phone with Mom simultaneously yelling away at him. To put an emphasis on her point, she would turn the blender on high (making the maximum amount of noise possible) in the kitchen and pretend that she had no idea that Dad was on the phone trying to put food on the table. Even to a young child, it was obvious to see the rudeness, stupidity, and complete lack of respect that was going on in our house. I recall after one such epic fight, I asked Dad why he stayed married to Mom if they did not like each other. I will always remember what he said in response, he simply stated "Son, your mother has many fine qualities." Nothing further. I will let the reader of this book determine the accuracy of this for themselves.

Once he was living in California, Dad would always drive a convertible (rag top) style car. He just could not get over how great it made him feel to have the warm breeze blow on his face as he relaxed and cruised slowly down the road. As he drove, Dad liked to tell stories of how he used to bet his New York friends that he could drive from one end of Manhattan to the other, without ever coming to a complete stop. He always won… driving as slowly and carefully so as not to hit any red lights or have to come to a complete stop was something he routinely did. He liked to compare life in California to how it was for him growing up in New York City. These were the only times I ever saw my father truly happy.

Dad also really liked to talk politics and social issues as well as play music. Either during dinner or in the evening sitting on the front lawn under the lemon tree, Dad would engage us (and our friends if they were around) in political discussions. He liked to hear our thoughts on the issues of the day and share his progressive views with us.

Then there was Dad's mandolin. This was Dad's prized instrument and he loved to strum the chords and occasionally sing along while he played. Sometimes, my sister, Randie would pick up a guitar and play along with Dad. Dad even wrote a few songs; his favorite song that he wrote was called "Surf Today" and it went something like this: "Surf today… the sun is shining bright. Waves are breaking far and rolling into sight. Grab your girl, take her by the hand. Run into the surf and paddle out from land. Surf today…"

Dad simply loved the music and the camaraderie of us kids. Late in his life he even went to the local community college and signed up for a singing class. He might not have ever known it, but there was not a class in the world that could have helped that poor man's singing. I should know… as I inherited his complete lack of musical ability. Thanks Dad.

Fred Shevin

Elaine Shevin (Mom)

Elaine was born in Brooklyn, New York and lived in Brighton Beach on the sixth floor of a six-story apartment building. She liked to tell us stories of "racing the elevator" by running up the stairs and always beating the elevator to the sixth floor. After graduating from high school Mom was full of resentment toward her own father as he sent her brother Stanley to college and not her. He said they did not have that much money and that girls didn't need an education because they were just going to get married and be homemakers anyhow; therefore it would be a waste of money. So Mom got a job in a department store (after school hours) and put herself through Teachers College in Columbia, eventually obtaining her teaching degree.

As time went on, Mom became unhappy with life in New York in general and moved away; first to Miami, Florida and then to California. Mom always wanted to be a doctor but let herself get talked out of it by a school counselor who said "women were nurses, not doctors." She then tried to become a news reporter but was told that women only wrote food and fashion columns, not the current events she was interested in covering. Next, Mom applied by mail for a job teaching Physical Education at Redlands University in California. She was 25 years old when she was invited to interview for that position and took a bus cross-country to meet with the college personnel office. At that meeting, she was asked what religion she practiced and when she answered "Jewish" she was told that she was the wrong religion and would not be hired for this job.

Since Mom was a good athlete she was guided towards a teaching position at Los Angeles Parks & Recreation Department teaching tennis and swimming, which she accepted and she taught for the next seven years. While living in Los Angeles, Mom met her future husband (my Dad) at a public dance. Dad "pursued Mom relentlessly" and eventually eloped in Las Vegas. Mom once told me, "this was a big mistake; we were not right for each other." However, they stayed married for companionship. As a newly married couple, they lived in a one room apartment "full of bugs and ants" so they could be close to Beverly Hills and the city for Dad to pursue his work connections in the movie industry. Mom and Dad remained married for 29 years until Dad passed away in 1979.

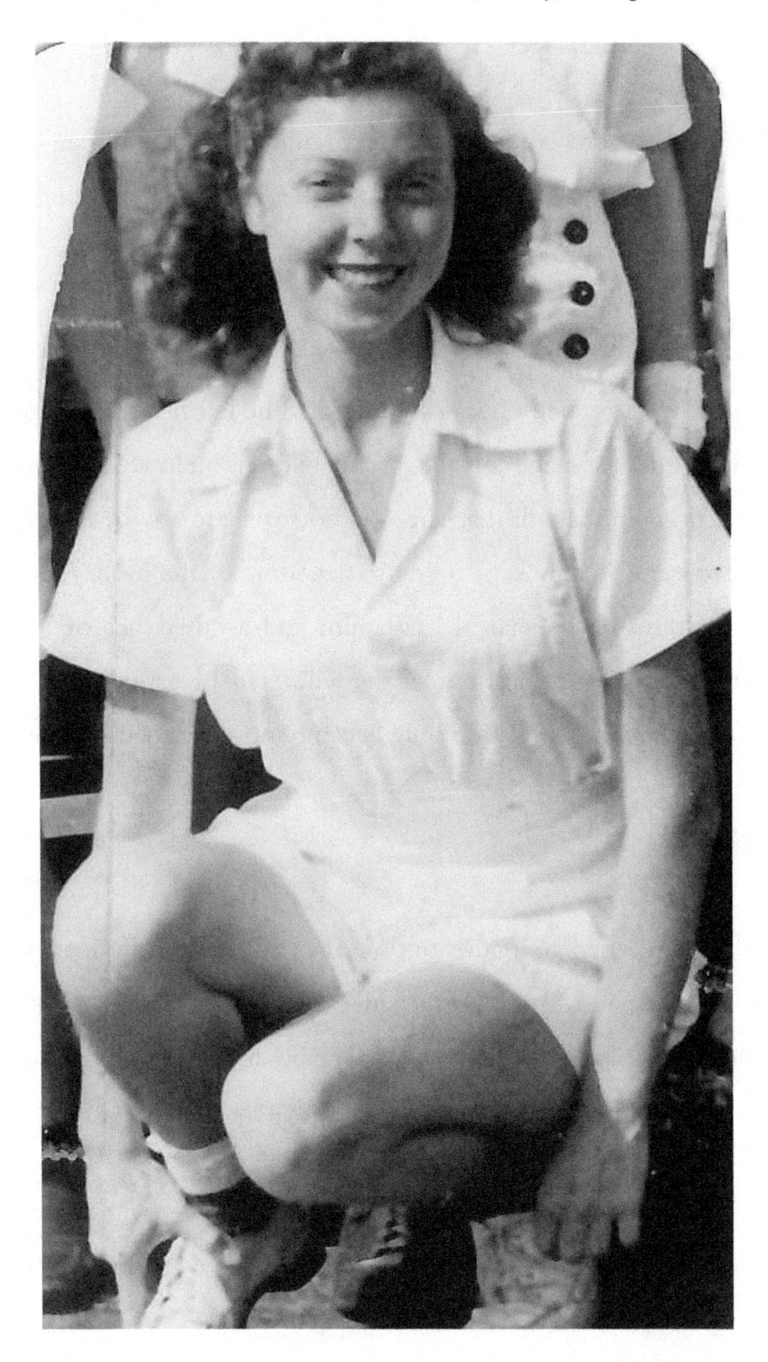

A Young Elaine

Mom was never very generous with either food or money. Maybe it was because she never had much of either. Maybe it was taught to her. We will never truly know.

I do know that when Grandpa Julius died he left her a small sum, along with a little for each of the grandchildren. However, he also left instructions in his will that she was not to share any of his estate with her brother. Stanley kept trying to get some of the money and blamed her for refusing to share it with him and accused her of influencing their father to write him out of the will. This put a tremendous strain on their relationship, which only became more strained and resentful as time marched forwards.

We all have tried to figure out WHEN Mom actually lost her mind. Was it the strain of raising four kids? Could it have been the strain of a difficult and loveless marriage? Maybe living through hard times? Maybe it was a combination of all of it that caused her to shift. We will never know… but shift she did.

Fred and Elaine

Fred and Elaine

Fred and Randie

The House

As I have said, my Dad grew up living in New York and as a boy dreamed of escaping from all of the snow and the biting cold. When he would play outside it was always on rooftops where he would never see a patch of green grass or a tree. So, when it was time to start raising a family of his own he decided to up and move to sunny California.

When he saw houses for sale in California with lush grass lawns and overflowing fruit trees, he thought that he had found heaven on earth. Surprisingly, he managed to buy a small house in the San Fernando Valley – Van Nuys to be exact.

Marc, Rory, and Randie in the Sunnyslope front yard

It was approximately 1,000 square feet on a small 8,640 square foot lot built in 1938. The house originally has three small bedrooms (which the six of us had to share and would constantly rotate rooms).

The house also only had one very small bathroom (for four growing kids and two adults) which became the location of our daily ritual fight to get a turn at the sink. I am describing the bathroom here so you will understand how I came to have a "*bathroom phobia*" later in life. First of all, like everything in the house, the bathroom was tiny and very old. The flooring was green and purple shag carpeting, badly soiled from years of damp footsteps coming out of the shower. It contained one small commode, a single sink with exposed plumbing, no cabinet or counters, and one very tiny pink tiled shower with dirt filled grout. Inside the shower was a single bare light bulb which turned on and off by pulling a string hanging down from the light. To this day I have no idea how none of us living there never electrocuted ourselves. Taking a shower was so disgusting that my little sister would only go in the shower if she was wearing sandals so she did not have to step on the tile. I think the goal of the shower was to get out as quickly as possible without touching anything, since it was so incredibly disgusting.

In later years the house would be expanded more than once. The first additions were another bedroom and full bathroom – which turned out to be strictly for Mom's use only. The remaining five of us would still have to fight over the single tiny, nasty, hall bath. The next addition was another small bedroom that was added for Randie, as she was a growing young lady and needed her own privacy. She actually paid for this bedroom addition herself, with money she had made from a few small acting parts. Over the years this room also provided a place for Grandpa to sleep when he visited, as well as a place for Dad to stay when Mom let him back in the house after they decided to try again after a breakup.

Amenities in the house were practically non-existent. There was one old fashioned rotary dial phone that Dad used for work that we all had to share. The tiny kitchen had one small sink, a tiny stove top, and a small refrigerator. There was no dishwasher, no air conditioner, no central heating, only a gas flame under-floor furnace in the living area, and a place for a washer and dryer in the detached garage.

Grandpa Jules and Baby Rory

Interestingly enough, in the back yard we had an incinerator where we took the trash to burn in an open air pit. Later in my childhood this method of trash disposal became outdated and trash was thereafter picked up by a trash man. After the trash was picked up, Dad tried to convince any one of us kids to pull the empty cans from the street back to the house by putting a coin under the empty can for us to find. That eventually stopped because he became frustrated by our lack of interest as we never "found" the coins he left.

Mom (Elaine), Rory, and Randie

We were all given a rotating list of weekly chores to do, there was always work to be done as there was no such thing as gardeners or housekeepers in this world of ours. Since Marc was the older boy he got to pick first and always chose mowing the grass. At the beginning he had to use an old style push mower (which took a lot of strength) but that was eventually replaced by a gas mower and tree trimmer (for the bushes and trees). I was always stuck picking up the trimmings – which I felt was just one of the harder chores I seemed to always get stuck with. I also had to cut back all of the ivy that grew around the property fence line. I would constantly try to trade chore jobs with my other siblings but no one was ever willing to trade with me and I was always stuck with these weekly activities. In addition to the outdoor chores we all had to take turns washing the dinner dishes each night. My sister Randie had to sweep the patios of fallen leaves, weed the yard, and water the gardens. We were all required to also work the seasonal apricot trees (which I will talk about shortly).

Stacey still likes to tell the story about the time she and I were told to pull all the weeds that were growing in the cracks in the patio and we nearly set the house on fire! Keep reading for that story.

Randie and Marc and Chubby Baby Rory

After a full day's activities we would all sit in the family room to watch TV together. Dad always got the prime spot on the sofa where he liked to lay out with his legs bent up to make room for one of us to sit, but whoever sat in the seat next to Dad's feet was always in the "firing zone." Mom would go into "her" room and leave everyone else to get a seat on the floor or by the floor furnace on cool nights. We had a small black and white TV box with three channels of reception, but only if the wire hanger antenna held the signal. There was no remote control, so if anyone wanted to change the channel or adjust the volume, they would have to get up off the floor or the couch each time. I liked to sit on the sofa next to my little sister and gently poke her in the arm until she would finally cry out, "stop poking me!" I think I may have been looking for some friendly attention as we spent our evenings together. Stacey still reminds me of this to this very day. This was our home.

Dad swimming with us in our "dough boy" pool

Marc, Randie and Rory playing in the back yard

Chubby Rory as a baby

The Four (Randie, Marc, Rory, Stacey)

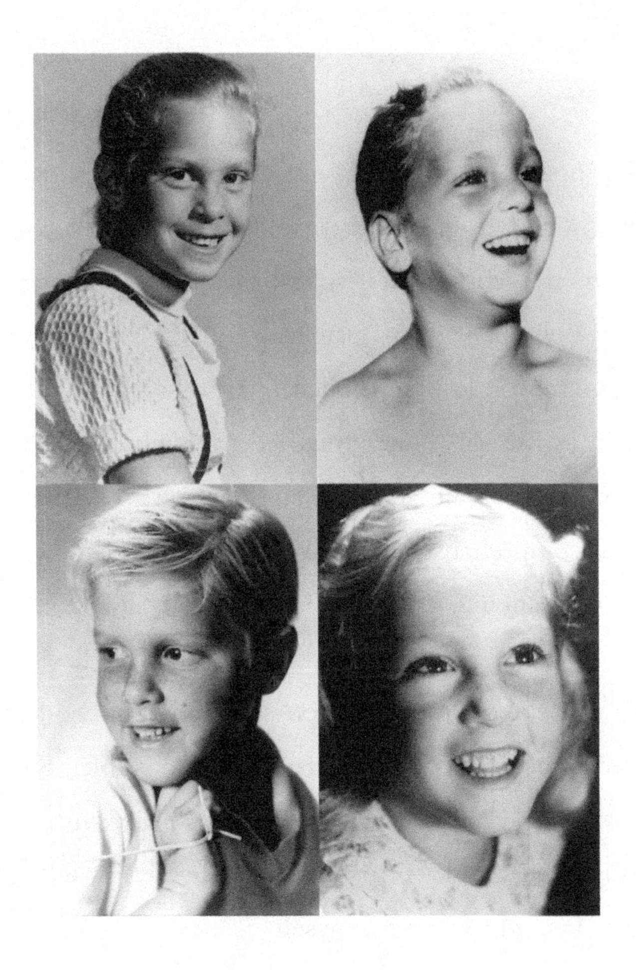

Parents always want their children to succeed. Part of what that meant to my Mom and Dad was they wanted their children to graduate from college, as that was an opportunity they were not given as children. Mom and Dad got their wish since they did get to see all four of their children graduate from college.

That did not mean that my siblings got away from the parental machine. Long before college my older sister Randie, was a swimming star and then a competitive volleyball player. She was on the U.S. Women's Volleyball Team just prior to our country boycotting the Olympic Games in 1980 for political purposes, the year the games were to be held in Russia. Randie married her high school sweetheart and then went on to obtain an EdD. and became an author, most notably publishing comprehensive inclusive curriculum "*Teaching Unity*" on the Oneness of Mankind, as well as lighter poetry books like "*Yes I'll Still Love You When You're Bald*". Chatting with Randie later in life she admitted that she did everything possible to get out and away from our unhealthy home environment as fast as was possible. She had planned to leave once she turned the legal age of 18 but simply couldn't wait. By the time she was 17 she was gone. She always felt remorseful for leaving me behind to fend for myself.

Marc and Rory in High School

My older brother Marc took mercy upon me… he took me along with him to the beaches and taught me to surf the waves. This gave me a much needed respite from our home life. For this, I will always owe him mightily. Marc was always the tough guy. He grew fast and strong and was never one to back off from a bully. As a teenager he told our mother, "I will never let you hit one of us again." Marc found a way out of this do or die parental machine by growling back at Mom's demands, by refusing to follow the commands, or by just disappearing for an entire summer on his friend's boat and fending for himself by working as a bus boy at a restaurant.

As Marc grew, he became a top ranked badminton player and later emerged as a pre-eminent residential real estate broker of his time, setting record after record and changing the landscape of Calabasas, California and the Hidden Hills area around him.

Stacey in High School

Randie just after high school at her wedding

My younger sister Stacey became a champion swimmer. At the time, she set and held both national and world records in her age group. She was also swimming in the Junior Olympics. Stacey was made to train in the pool six days a week, often two times per day – once very early before school began and once again after school. On Sundays she would have to run miles on the track, do strength training with weights on pulleys set up for her at the house, and study Mom's notes on her progress. This included listening to Mom read her notes from a legal pad to and from the pool. When Stacey complained about being overly exhausted, Mom simply would not listen. Not long after, Stacey succumbed to a ferocious bout of mononucleosis forcing her to become bedridden for a full year and a second year of home rest. I believe this was all due to the intense pressure from our Mom to succeed at all costs. As soon as Stacey was back on her feet, Mom said, "great, now we can get you back into training." Stacey could barely raise the necessary energy to tell Mom, "no more!"

Now, Stacey still swims at 60+ years of age, setting world age records at Masters events and doing long distance ocean swimming (such as swimming 24 miles from Catalina Island to the mainland, from the Channel Islands to the mainland and around Alcatraz, plus many more such notable achievements). She was training to swim across Lake Tahoe until the 2021 fires shut the swim down.

Stacey with her "swimmers" hair (pre swim cap days)

In our home, we traded bedrooms and switched off who we shared the bedroom with. I remember when I shared rooms with Randie, we would lie in bed in the evenings and make up stories by taking turns adding to the story one sentence at a time. The story usually had a Mom (known as *The Witch*) that ended up crashing as she chased us down. We thought that was the funniest thing ever and would retell the story and scream with laughter for years after. Other favorite games included taking turns naming a food until we got too tired to continue (I think we were obsessed with food, but I will get to that).

It was different when Marc and I took turns at sharing a room. We were both growing and developing our own styles. Marc liked things clean, neat, and orderly. I was learning to enjoy surfing and loved music posters with black lights shining on them. We fought and argued over which person should get to have the room the way we liked it best. We ended up agreeing to put a line of tape down the middle of the room and we could each decorate our side of the room as we liked it. After putting the tape on the floor, we quickly realized I would have to walk across Marc's side to get to my side of the room. After much thought we decided there was nothing that could be done and we would have to make the best of it, which is what we did.

That left Stacey with no one to share a room with. Our house also had a very unusual design, thanks to the additions, which required going through Stacey's bedroom as the only way to get to Mom's room. I can clearly remember that the rest of us wanted nothing to do with Mom walking back and forth through our room as she pleased so we were all willing to let Stacey have that room alone while the rest of us took turns sharing a room with one another.

This only served to emphasize for the rest of us siblings that Stacey was the favorite and got favored treatment from Mom. In fact, the rest of us grew to become rather jealous of Stacey as we felt she had quite a few privileges the rest of us did not have. These not only included her having her own room but also going to a private school for one year (something our Dad apparently got for some PR work he did for the school), but also a lighter chore list which gave her more time for outside activities like horseback riding lessons, more food to eat, and (horrors!) even being taken shopping for new clothes. At one point this escalated to the point that we locked Stacey in a small closet in the entry to the house where she stayed for the entire day until Mom inquired about her whereabouts as dinner time approached. Stacey did not know what was worse, the potential wrath of her siblings or the potential wrath of Mom. In retrospect, being the favorite of Mom was not necessarily easier, Stacey still got the "Mom machine" when it came to swimming and suffered as well. But as a kid caught in my web of beatings and acting and hunger, I did not see that at the time.

Randie and Marc at the beach

In the patio, each summer we would blow up a small "Dough Boy" inflatable pool that held about one foot or so of water (see photo earlier in this book). Mom would get the first turn, she would tie an elastic band around her ankle so that she could swim in place for (what seemed like) hours at a time. When Mom finally gave us a turn, Dad would lie in the shallow pool and pretend he was a whale and us kids were minnows. As we took turns jumping into the water we squealed as Dad tried to catch us. These were fun times.

When we needed more adventure, we all had bicycles that we would race around the neighborhood. As I grew, I asked Dad if I could buy a mini-bike with some of the money I had earned from acting. He agreed and helped me buy a Bonanza (motorized mini bike) which gave me hours of pleasure riding around. It was amazing that I did not kill myself, which became apparent even to me after I had one close call after another. I ended up selling the motorbike to live for another day.

Dad enjoying the four of us at the pool (note our expressions)

Sugar (the dog)

Sugar, a Boxer, was our family pet. She lived on our outdoor patio and slept under where the BBQ would go on cold nights. I have never before (or since) seen a dog run like she ran. On days that Mom would take the family to the park, she would load the car up with all the kids and then close the car doors so Sugar was on the outside of the car. As we slowly started to drive, we would call and whistle and yell for Sugar to run after the car. She really seemed to like the running. Mom would drive just fast enough so if Sugar was running at full stride, we could just keep her in sight running behind the car. Sugar would run so fast, cutting across people's lawns or cutting the corner, so she could stay up with the car as we all continued to yell for her. I don't know how we never had any problem with traffic or cars, but I guess it was just a different time. Sugar was always ready to go! She would wait on the patio for her name to be called… and off she would run.

She was so sweet and we all loved her so! I will always remember one night Mom gave me a single, plain, hamburger patty for my entire dinner (as she wanted me to diet). I was so upset and hungry that I took my little patty outside and sat down on the step to eat my little meal. Sugar came over (of course) and whispered to me to see if she could just have a taste as she was hungry too. So I broke the little patty in half and shared my dinner with Sugar. We both went to bed hungry that night but possibly a little bit happier.

When Sugar got older she got into a dogfight, lost badly, and got really torn up by the other dog. Mom said she had a huge gash on her side where a big piece of flesh had been torn off. Mom took Sugar away and left her collar, with her name on it, on the table where everyone would see it. She never told us exactly what happened or if Sugar had died, she simply left the collar out there for us to see and come to our own conclusions.

Mom eventually (years later) told Randie that she took Sugar to the vet and had her put to sleep, since we could not afford to pay for surgery for a dog. A very sad day indeed.

Eric (the cat)

Eric was a striking Siamese with short white fur, grey markings, and bright blue eyes. He was smart as could be and loved to entertain us. In the evenings, when we would all sit in the living room after dinner, Eric would climb up on his cat tree (which reached from floor to ceiling) and do acrobatics for us. There was a hole cut out in the upper platform which Eric could do flips and tumbles through. In between his tricks he would race up and down then stop for bows as we all hooted and cheered in amazement. *What cat does this stuff?* ... we would all wonder aloud. But there was something else Eric would do as well. After the "main show" was over, he would climb over to the sofa, find a comfortable spot sitting on someone's lap, and then began to masturbate. Seriously. YUK! We would all yell, "EW! What's that?!" and push him away. He would never be deterred though. He would just come right back to the couch, find someone else to sit on, and continue right along as if no one had objected. He would keep making pleasurable sucking sounds and knead the blanket or pillows with his claws until he was done pleasuring himself. Like I said, what cat does this stuff?!

Now we come to my story

Shocking, Unbelievable, Hard to Understand, But all true. Every Word.

One of my first solid memories as a toddler was being left at the park. My mother liked to play tennis at the local neighborhood park and on tennis days Mom would put me in the sandbox located on the other side of the park until she was finished. One such tennis day as dinner approached, someone asked her "Where is Rory?" After looking all over the house and yard, Mom realized that she must have left me at the park playing in the sandbox. She raced back to the park only to find me in the exact same spot in the sandbox where I was placed early that same morning. I was the easy little boy… easy to manipulate, easy to control, easy to make into whatever they wanted. A Money Machine.

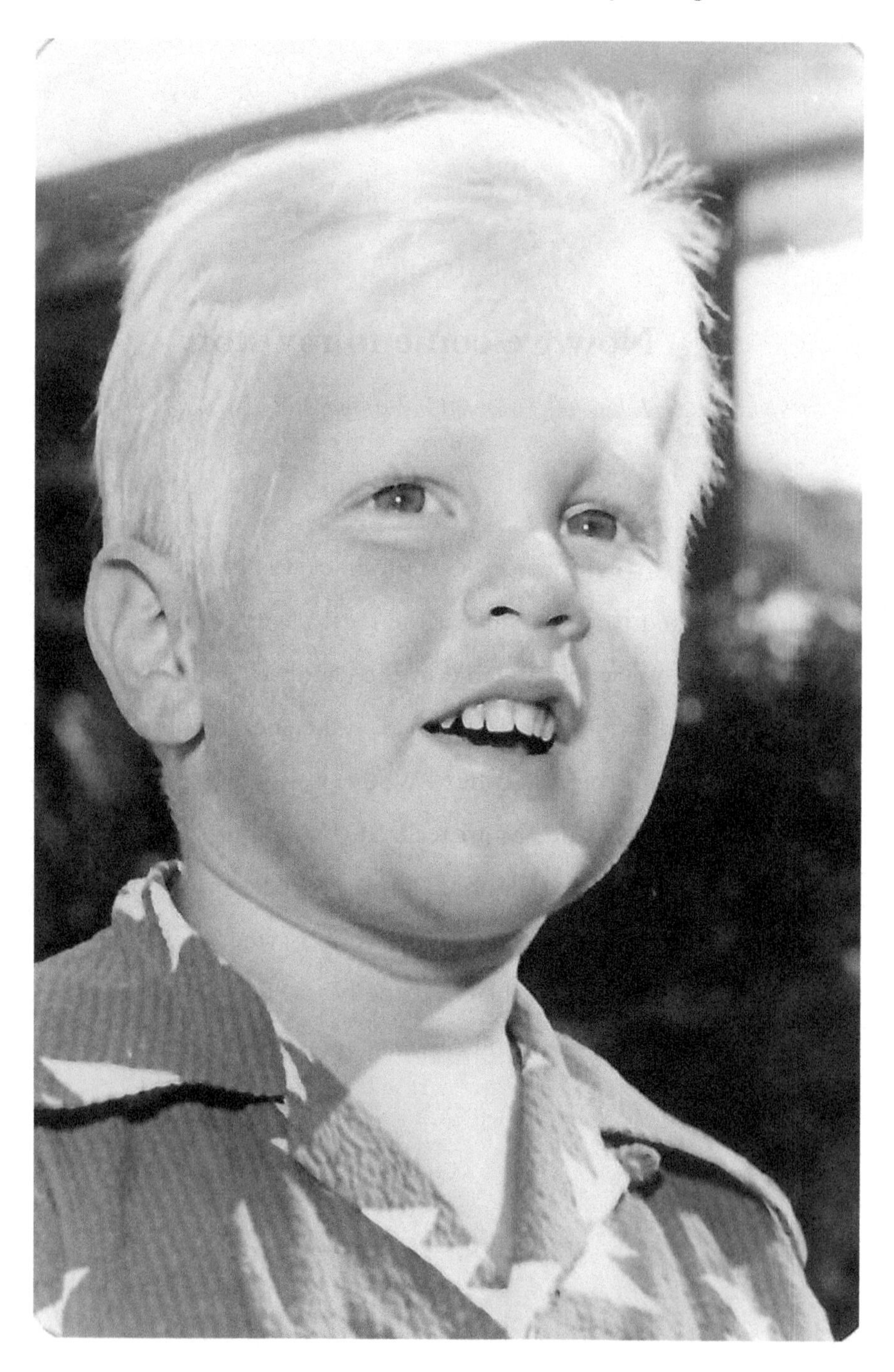

Young Rory

Then it all started. Like previously I mentioned, Mom and Dad had decided my future and my fate without ever considering what I wanted. I was to become a child actor. By the time I was five years young, I was having professional photo sessions in our home to get the perfect headshots. I still have a wealth of photos with smears of dirt and makeup across my face to create the "certain look" they were going for. By the time I was six, the commercials started coming in for me. Oscar Meyer Hot Dogs, Lays Potato Chips, Clairol Hair Products, Crest Tooth Paste, Skippy Peanut Butter, and so many more.

Mom and Dad wanted me to have "the look"… whatever that was. They wanted my hair to stay light/white blonde, so they squeezed lemon juice on my hair at night while I was forced to lean over the bathtub and endure the stinging juice. One evening while struggling over the tub receiving my juice treatment, somehow I slipped and chipped my front tooth on the bathtub. Oh no. While I liked the new chipped-tooth look, my parents were horrified and rushed me off to the dentist to have my tooth drilled down to a nub and a cap placed over the chipped tooth. Now I can act again they said. This simple incident has caused me a lifetime of dental chair visits and work on that tooth. They wanted me to be slender, which meant putting me on strict diets forevermore. Bottom line was they wanted my looks not to change at all, not to grow taller or fatter or bigger, to keep my hair lighter and keep the same look that was bringing success… to keep the acting and commercial work coming in… and it was working!

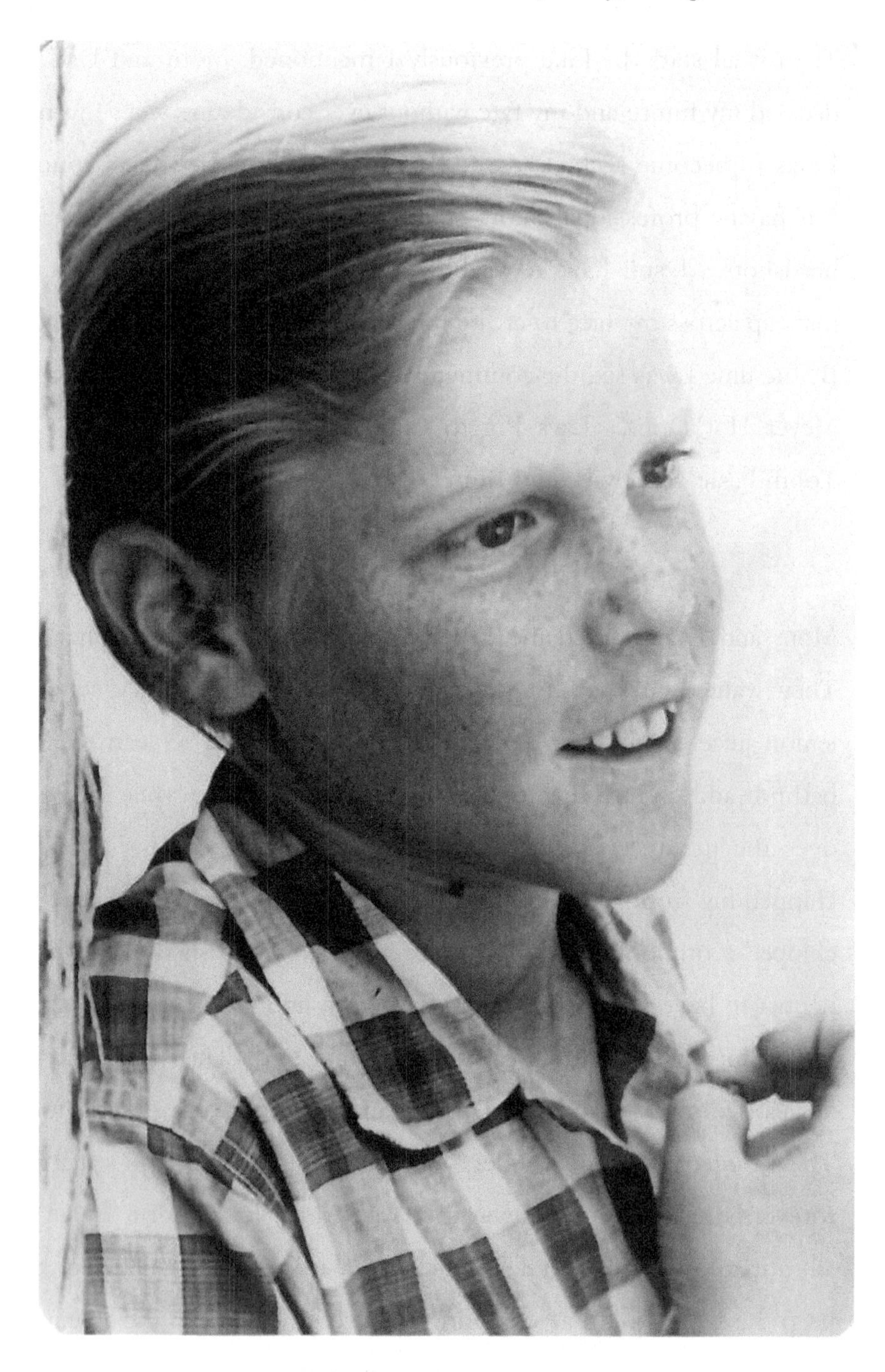

However, as I grew Mom saw I was getting a little pudgy (as is normal for a growing child) and decided to restrict my diet to keep me thin. I was destined to become a 6'4" man and they did not realize nor care that they were starving me and stunting my growth. On the way home from one of our late nights filled with interviews, Mom passed an apple to me saying that this single apple would be my dinner tonight and when we got home she put me straight to bed. Dad heard this and apparently felt bad. I will always remember him sneaking a piece of cheese into my bedroom later that night in his pajama pocket so Mom would never know.

Mom became fixated on keeping me thin and would not allow me to eat any food that was not given to me by her. We all walked to elementary school those days (which was about two miles from home). Being hungry (as we all were since she would not allow my siblings to eat either), we took to looking in people's trash cans for things to eat along the way. Also, there were a few large walnut trees growing along the path to school and, when in season, we would pick and eat the nuts. When I arrived home at the end of each school day Mom would put me on a scale and weigh me to see if I gained any weight (which would tell her if I was cheating on her food rules and finding food to eat). Some days the scale would show gains and I would cry and promise I had not cheated by eating anything. Mom would then inspect my teeth to try and determine if I had food bits stuck in my teeth or not. I was checked, threatened, and beaten with a leather belt on a regular basis if

Mom thought I was eating any scrap of food she had not sent with me to school.

One additional thing I had forgotten about but my sister Randie reminded me, to be extra thorough Mom got some type of special paste from the dentist. If you rubbed this paste on your teeth and gums it turned a pinkish color to show where little bits of food were lurking. It was intended to be a dental aid to promote better tooth brushing but Mom used it to see if we were eating anything. The battle continued… and we continued to be hungry all the time.

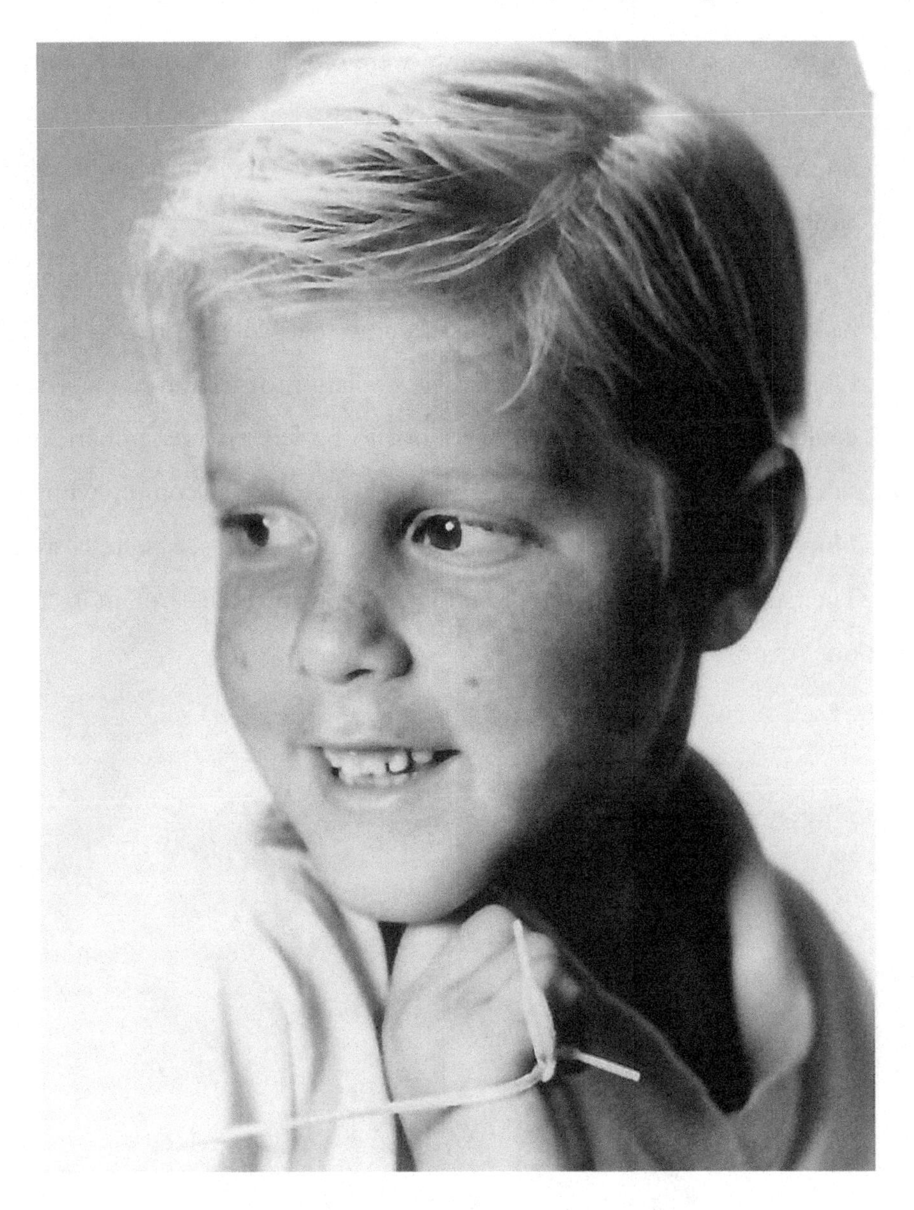

There were times in our lives when friends from school or from the neighborhood asked if we could come over to play. This was always interesting for us as we liked to brainstorm how Mom was going to be able to stop us from eating when we were out of her immediate control. We were actually excited to have a chance to get a treat at our friend's house where Mom would never know about it. As it turned out, when treat time did come around our friend's mothers would tell us that they would love to give us whatever treat they were having but our mother had called in advance and let them know that we were not to be fed. Our mother would claim we were sick, allergic, or whatever excuse she could make up to ensure we were not to be fed. It was embarrassing since no one really believed her, but felt they should comply with our Mom's request so they did not upset things while we were visiting. Their discomfort with this situation resulted in the loss of more than one friendship for me.

Walking to elementary school with a strong hunger inside our bellies we looked inside people's trash cans (usually on trash day) as we made our way to school. We often found things to nibble on… until one day we hit the jackpot. Stacey lifted the cover of a can and stacked up nice and neat (and still warm in their sealed boxes) were five boxes of fresh warm pies right there on top. That was a glorious day! We all ate until our tummies were full. I will never know what caused that home owner to throw those beautiful pies away but we never felt so lucky… and it never happened again. From that day on, and just to be silly, we gave Stacey the nick name Five Pie!

As I briefly touched on earlier, Mom and Dad fought loudly and consistently over the food shopping… which was done by Mom and only once a week. Dad gave Mom an $80.00 allowance for the full week's shopping for four growing children and two adults. He was convinced that was adequate and Mom was probably "stealing" some of the money for herself. So the battles continued. Mom pulled out receipts from the store and challenged Dad to come do the shopping himself. Before leaving for the store each week, Mom cut out coupons from as many stores as she could find to help spread out the money she had for the week's amount of food. Mom always complained there was no way she was actually saving anything when you add in the cost of gas and her time driving all over town. Over time, as costs increased Mom had to ask Dad for $100.00 for the week's shopping, the battles and screaming just increased right along with the prices. One week

Mom brought home a quart of apple juice (since she knew I liked juice). I took the jar and drank it down to the bottom within a few seconds before Mom could see what I had done. When Mom saw the empty jar she went crazy with rage, saying that was to last for the full week. This incident was probably the cause of Mom starting to label all the food in the refrigerator as to whom it was for and who was not allowed to touch it (more on that later). This spread even further to the freezer in our garage being secured with chains and locks (which is another story I will get to later in this book). This led to many epic battles of who ate what when it was not allowed by Mom.

Through all of this, my Dad seemed to maintain his good sense of humor and seemed to enjoy his kids and his life. Dad entertained himself by giving people he talked to different or funny sounding names based on what kind of letters or meanings or rhymes he could make up. For example, when anyone called on the phone for us Dad would leave us an encrypted message with their names in code that we would have to figure out what he was meaning. When our friends, the Nestles down the street called he might leave a message saying something like "Nestles chocolate called for us." Or the one time we went to a department store to buy a winter coat and the sales lady in the coat department, by some strange coincidence, was actually named Mrs. Coats. Dad had a field day with that one. By the time Dad was done teasing her, she honestly didn't seem sure if she worked there or not.

We would try to get back at Dad for all the games he played on us by hiding or eating the food he was making for himself for breakfast. What usually happened was, when Dad was preparing his breakfast, he would get a work call and have to take the phone. At this time I would either eat his toast he had been toasting or just take his plate and hide it somewhere so he would have to find it.

Even with all of the food fights and silly games I tried my best to have a normal childhood in between all of my acting jobs. At one point I decided that I wanted to play Little League Baseball. I loved the Dodgers and listened to them in bed each night they played, as often as I could during baseball season, on a little AM radio I had. Mom said if I wanted to play baseball I would have to ride my bike to the park on my own (about 3-4 miles each way) as she had no time to drive me. So that is exactly what I did for many years. I loved it. I was short and pudgy, but I was a good fielder and could hit the ball, but couldn't run a lick. My brother used to say I could stretch a home run into a single.

Mom, however, wanted me to be a tennis star. After giving me lessons herself for many years she signed me up for professional lessons. We had to drive downtown to the pro's court which used up whatever free time I had left. So when I told Mom I had had enough and did not want to play tennis, she said I could get a college scholarship with tennis if I only stuck to it. Honestly at that young age I didn't even understand what that meant.

At this point in my child acting career, I was getting one commercial job after another. My agent kept sending me on one interview after another and, for whatever the reason, I kept getting the jobs. At one point I was featured in more than six commercials running on TV at the same exact time. The advertisers started calling my agent to ask them not to send me out on any more interviews for commercials for a while as they felt I was over-saturating the airways with too many product endorsements. Spanning the 15-20 years of my acting work, I figure I was in approximately 100 different commercials. It is hard to be more specific as I have searched for records of the commercials I was in but have been told that no one keeps records of commercials – only TV shows and motion pictures. As to those photos and records, only my Mom would ever know what really happened… as you will read shortly.

100 years of know-how goes out the door with every pair.
LILLEHAMMER
bratlie
bratlie
bratlie
Today's know-how is fiberglass strength and the STEP-TEX waxless base.
When you've been making nordic equipment this long, you have a big advantage. Experience has moved SKILOM from a great tradition in wood skis to extra strength, high performance, fiberglass models. There's 100 years of know-how in our new STEP-TEX base, too. No other ski will give you our "kick" and long glide, without wax! For *any* cross-country item, count on SKILOM for know-how and performance. 100 years ahead in skis, boots, bindings, poles, waxes and cross-country accessories.
Send $1.00 for Skilom's illustrated introduction to nordic skiing: A&T Ski Company, 455 Andover Park East, Seattle, WA, 98188. Or see your local Skilom dealer.
SKILOM
A&T SKI

Acting Parts: Age 6-9 years young

1960 - 1963

By the time I was six years young, in the early 1960's, my list of credits grew substantially. I was signed to act in five episodes of the *Leave it to Beaver Show* with the recurring role of the character "Chucky Murdoch" (Beaver's neighbor). This included a feature role in the episode "Chuckie's New Shoes." This easily recognized role, in this iconic TV show, really set the stage for my acting career to take hold… which it did.

Leave it to Beaver, "Chuckie's New Shoes." 1960 -1962

In this episode, I worked with stars Tony Dow, Jerry Mathers as the Beaver, as well as Hugh Beaumont and Barbara Billingsley (the Beaver's parents). At the time I was six years old and looked closer to four years of age. In this classic scene, which somehow seemed to apply directly to my home life, we had the following dialogue which says it all. Chuckie said that "he was scared that his mother was going to hit him for being bad." Chuckie's Mom responded with, "When does Mommy ever hit you for no reason?" Chuckie comes back with emphasis, "ALL THE TIME!" *As you will read later about my home life, having my Mom hitting me for reasons (or no reasons) was a common thread of my upbringing. It is nothing short of amazing that the dialogue in this scene mirrored my home life to the T.*

Other episodes of Leave it to Beaver that I had roles in included:

"Wally the Business Man" 5/28/1960 season 3 episode 35.

In this scene, Wally was selling ice cream as a street vendor. Chuckie talked Wally into giving him two ice cream bars (one for him and one for his sister at home). Then, without paying, Chuckie took a large bite of the ice cream before Wally could take them back. I promised to pay for them the next day but when Wally came the next day I told him I did not know what he was talking about and said I had never seen him before. *This must have been extraordinarily exciting for me as I was never allowed to eat ice cream bars in my real home life.*

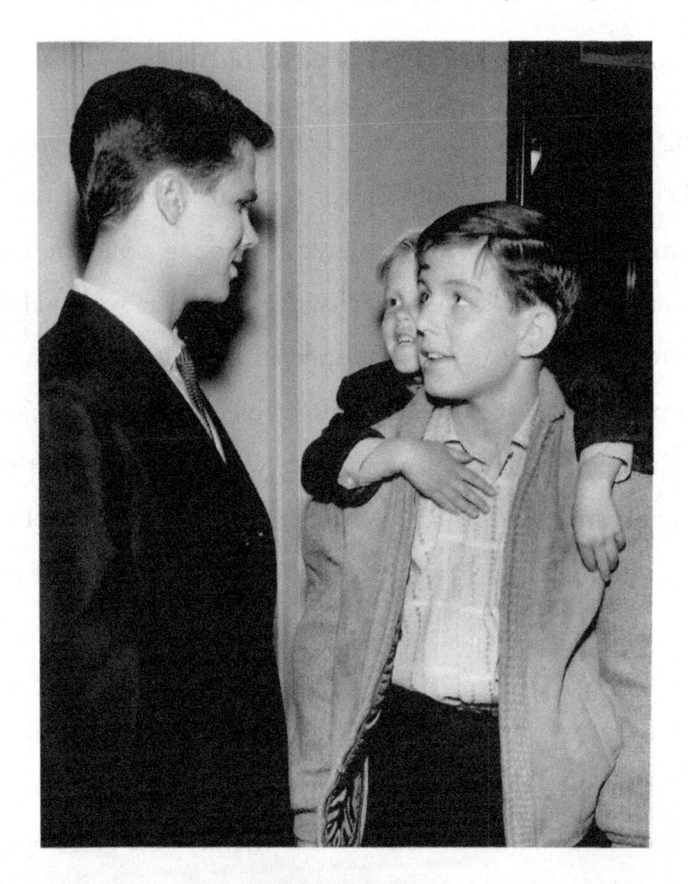

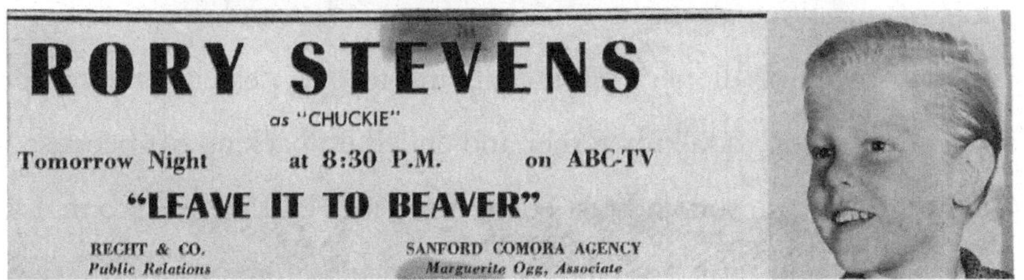

"Beavers Frogs" 5/2/1961 season 4 episode 35

"Beaver the Babysitter" 4/2/1962 season 5 episode 27

Bonanza "The Legacy" 1963 (9 years old) *CD*

Staring Lorne Greene, Michel Landon, Pernell Roberts, and Dan Blocker (as Hoss). I will always remember working on the classic western, BONANZA. I warmly recall working alongside Dan Blocker (who starred as Hoss). I had one long scene with "Hoss" as my character "Danny Page." Hoss showed himself to be a very kind and warm person. I felt safe and comfortable working with him and have always remembered him warmly, since we worked together when I was just nine years old. The scene had extensive dialogue and I am amazed that as a nine year old I could remember all that and handle such a task.

In this episode, I played the son of a suspect in the possible killing of Ben Cartwright. Hoss comes to my house to investigate my father and finds me home alone. I tried to make friends with Hoss by asking him lots of questions about how he knew my father and even inviting him to stay over for dinner. Hoss tells me to "go pester someone else." Hoss was going to kill my father and ended up backing off because "my father had a cute son and just couldn't do it." During this scene, I went up to Hoss and took his hand to try to get his attention. All these years later I remember holding his hand and thinking how huge his hands were (see the photo). For years I kept photos of us doing this scene together on the wall of my home. This is one of the very few mementos I have saved and actually put up for display in my home.

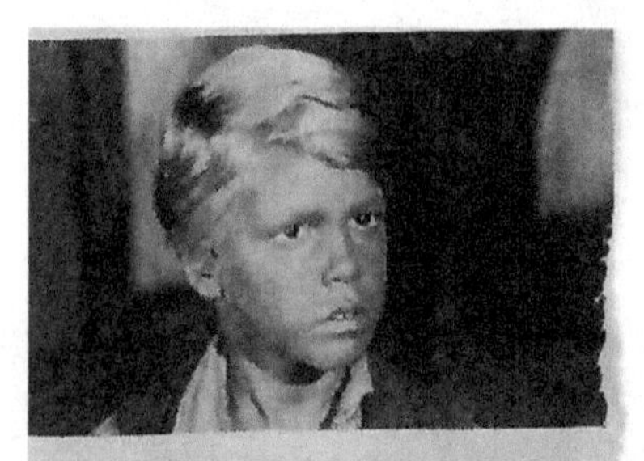

RORY STEVENS

"BONANZA"—Dec. 15

"ARREST & TRIAL"—Dec. 22

Just Completed — (Pilot)

"MR. HANNAN & THE LITTLE PEOPLE"

Now Shooting — "GRINDL"

Rep.: MARCELLA BELL AGENCY

AVANTI '63

Perfect Condition

10,000 miles. 4-speed transmission. Supercharger. All power.

$4,000

Call HO 9-9011, Ext. 32 weekdays

MINK FOR CHRISTMAS

Beautiful three-quarter length coat with rich, dark color and magnificent high styling. Natural blocked skins. Circular with 52" sweep. Very nearly new. Sacrifice at ½ price.

$2,750 cash EXbrook 4-7189

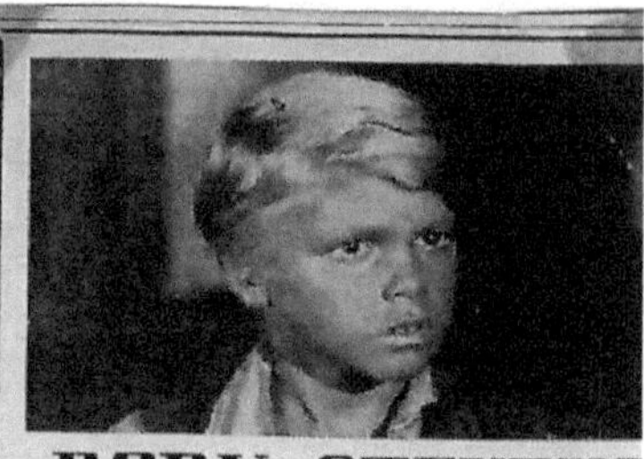

RORY STEVENS

"BONANZA" — Dec. 15

"ARREST & TRIAL"—Dec. 22

Just Completed — (Pilot)

"MR. HANNAN & THE LITTLE PEOPLI

Now Shooting — "GRINDL"

Rep.: MARCELLA BELL AGENCY

Andy Griffith Show "Andy and Opie Housekeepers" 1961 (7 years old) *On Amazon Prime*

Staring Andy Griffith, Don Knotts, and Ron Howard (as Opie).

In this scene with Ron Howard as Opie, I had come over to his house to play. However, Opie was supposed to clean up his very messy room before playing…But we got silly making a huge mess jumping on the bed like it was a trampoline (which I had at my real home). What a nice guy and true class act Ron Howard is and was... and what deserved success he had with his life in show business.

Wagon Train "The Nancy Palmer Story" 1961 (7 years old) *On YouTube*

As I looked back through time to being only seven years old and looked not a day over five, I could not believe how small and young I looked and the high squeaky voice that I had. It felt like the twilight zone.

Next followed rolls in:

Dr. Kildare, (Season 1, Episode 7, 1961) The Lonely Ones, McKeever and the Colonel, (Season 1, Episode 9, 1962) Blackwells Stand, Alcoa

Premiere, (1963), General Electric Theater (1963), The Dyke Van Show, The Joey Bishop Show, The Lloyd Bridges Show, The Sam Benedict Show, (Season 1, Episode 24, 1962-63) 17 Gypsies and a Sinner Named Charlie, Going My Way, Murder Me, Arrest and Trial, Morning Court, The Untouchables. Most notably was Alfred Hitchcock's, The Birds, as mentioned previously. The work kept on coming and I kept on working, plus doing multiple interviews for each of the parts I got. The more shows I did, the more other directors and producers wanted to interview me for their shows.

Eddy Mayhoff as the father
Rory Stevens as the son
in "How To Murder Your Wife"

The commercial products and television roles continued to mount while life at home became more and more like a bad horror show.

Whenever I had an interview, Mom liked to tell me to say specific things (whether it was applicable to the conversation I was having or not). She said this would make the interviewers remember me. Mom said I was not allowed to come out of the interview unless I had said the arranged topic. As I came out of the interview room, Mom would quickly ask if I had said the thing she gave me to say (for example), "you know I went horseback riding yesterday" or "I'm getting close to beating my Mom at tennis now." It made no sense as it had nothing to do with what we were talking about, and I felt it made me look dumb. Often I had used the sentence but sometimes I just would not be able to. Sometimes the interview was very short as the producer/director (or casting agent) already knew what they had in mind for the role and would dismiss you quickly with a "thank you for coming out, goodbye." In these cases, I had no time to say the pre-arranged topic and Mom would insist that "I turn around and walk right back in the room and say it!" Keep in mind you were only allowed to enter the producer/directors room when called in. You're damn right this was incredibly awkward and embarrassing but that was what living with a show business Mom was like.

All the while, the auditions for commercials and acting jobs continued. Sometimes they turned out to be blessings in disguise. One time I interviewed for a Skippy Peanut Butter commercial. In the interview, they spread the peanut butter onto a slice of white bread and told me to take a bite. At the time, we were not allowed to eat white bread, only wheat, as Mom said white bread had no nutritional value. I was so thrilled to get something to eat! I didn't have to act or pretend. I shoved as much of the sandwich as far into my mouth as possible and then asked for more. I was SO EXCITED and I got the job.

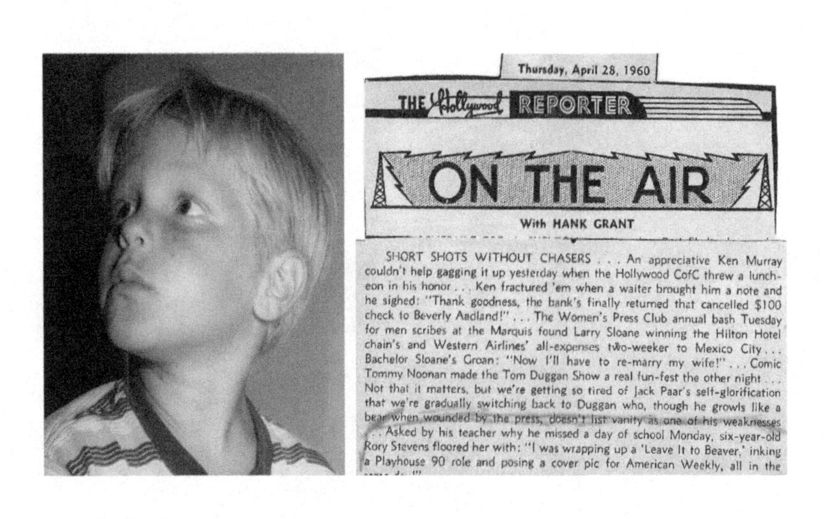

Thursday, April 28, 1960

THE Hollywood REPORTER

ON THE AIR

With HANK GRANT

SHORT SHOTS WITHOUT CHASERS . . . An appreciative Ken Murray couldn't help gagging it up yesterday when the Hollywood CofC threw a luncheon in his honor . . . Ken fractured 'em when a waiter brought him a note and he sighed: "Thank goodness, the bank's finally returned that cancelled $100 check to Beverly Aadland!" . . . The Women's Press Club annual bash Tuesday for men scribes at the Marquis found Larry Sloane winning the Hilton Hotel chain's and Western Airlines' all-expenses two-weeker to Mexico City . . . Bachelor Sloane's Groan: "Now I'll have to re-marry my wife!" . . . Comic Tommy Noonan made the Tom Duggan Show a real fun-fest the other night . . . Not that it matters, but we're getting so tired of Jack Paar's self-glorification that we're gradually switching back to Duggan who, though he growls like a bear when wounded by the press, doesn't list vanity as one of his weaknesses . . . Asked by his teacher why he missed a day of school Monday, six-year-old Rory Stevens floored her with: "I was wrapping up a 'Leave It to Beaver,' inking a Playhouse 90 role and posing a cover pic for American Weekly, all in the

Thanksgiving Dinner

The Thanksgiving holiday season became a place of abject embarrassment for us kids. Why? We were forced to watch Mom's bizarre behavior at the dinner table. To this day, all four of us kids have not been able to find an adequate explanation for why Mom did what she did. What did she do? It couldn't have been that odd, right? Well, to start with, Mom baked the turkey in a large brown paper bag. When it was done cooking, she would then slice all of the meat away from the bone and serve it to the family. Normal so far. However, when it came to serving herself she would say something like "Oh, I will just eat what's left on the bones." We all told Mom there was plenty of good meat for her to have but no she insisted, "I will eat this part so no one else has to worry." She would then sit at the table with the bag, proceeded to tear the bag wide open, lay the carcass out in front of her, and proceed to dig in and eat it like a starving animal – without utensils, using her hands, all the while grunting as she was tearing at the bones in pleasure, as she devoured one section of the carcass through to the last. On rare occasions when we were allowed to have a friend or other family member over for Thanksgiving dinner, we would beg them not to watch or pay any attention to our Mom as we had no explanation to offer them for her behavior.

Thanksgiving Celebrations Today

As the years went by, our Thanksgiving meal changed as the landscape of our family began to change. They started with crazy awkward meals (as I just described)… but with our family expanding year by year (marriages, babies, children, cousins, grandpas, grandmas, and so on), we just kept adding chairs to the table and getting more cozy as we went along. The last count at Thanksgiving this past year (2021) was 32 of us seated comfortably all over the house. We all love to go around the table taking turns telling stories and expressing what we are most thankful for that year. Sometimes these honestly make you cry, or breathe a sigh, and other times just laugh out loud. What a beautiful loving family we have all created over the years.

Thanksgiving in Yakima at Randie's house – one of the many cousins line ups

One such story that gets told time and again was the time all the grandchildren and cousins were over at Mom's house for Thanksgiving. Mom offered everyone a frozen banana shake which sounded great to all the kids. Keep in mind that at this time in Mom's life, her eyesight had been declining for some time. With that in mind, Mom went to the freezer and pulled out (what she thought was) the frozen bananas… only to quickly discover that the bananas were not bananas at all but raw frozen chicken. Mom had made raw frozen chicken shakes. Everyone was screaming and gagging and never let Mom make any food from that point on. She even ground up the bones in the blender!

A Few Other "Fun" Food Stories

Stacey likes to tell the story about the time she came home from college for summer vacation. She wanted some ice cream and went to the freezer where she found a carton eaten half way down. After eating for a while, she decided to finish off the box. However, she felt the need to replace this so she went to the store and bought a carton of the same kind of ice cream, and brought it home. Then realizing she had to eat the ice cream down to the same level she originally found the first box to be in, she got to work. She enjoyed this treat so much she couldn't stop, and finished off the second box. Without hesitating she went back to the store for a third carton, which she again brought home and had to eat half way down (where she originally started with the first carton) so as not to get in trouble with Mom.

Another one of Stacey's favorite stories when she was a child was the time she found where Mom kept the dog's supply of Milk Bone Biscuit treats. After trying a few nibbles, she decided that they were crunchy and even decently yummy. So whenever the coast was clear, she would sneak a biscuit from the kitchen and hide it in her closet so she would have a stash of dog biscuits for snacks whenever she got hungry. Believe it or not, I found out later that all four of us kids did this same thing!

Another memorable favorite was one of the times we actually had a friend come over to hang out with us. This poor friend had never seen a kitchen full of labels with every ones name on each individual piece of food. She became hysterical with laughter and began putting labels with different people's names on everything, not only in the refrigerator, but the whole kitchen and all through the house. They laughed so long and so hard they cried huge tears of laughter as they went labeling things throughout the house.

Casting Calls

On any typical day at elementary school I would be called into the principal's office to find my Mom or Dad waiting there to take me out of school and into Hollywood for another interview. Or, more commonly, Mom would send the school a note to make sure I was ready to meet her right after class as she had acting job interviews lined up. These interviews could include anything from cattle calls (which meant huge numbers of people applying for the part), to call backs (which was when the number of people was whittled down to just a few) which ramped up the excitement factor.

12—B'NAI B'RITH MESSENGER
Friday, April 15, 1966

Valley Youth Has Busy TV Schedule

RORY STEVENS — who, at 11, is one of the busiest television stars in the Valley. He's just added the role of a robot in "The Munsters" to his growing list of credits which includes Gomer Pyle, Jesse James, Bewitched, Please Don't Eat the Daisies, The Virginian, Bonanza, My Favorite Martian and others plus many major commercials. Rory attends the Erwin Street School in Van Nuys.

VALLEYWIDE-One of the busiest TV stars in the Valley is 11 year old Rory Stevens, who when he isn't attending the Erwin Street School in Van Nuys, is generally working on some TV show or motion picture.

Just this past week, he played a lead, a robot, no less on an episode of very popular

RORY STEVENS

series, "The Munsters" the title of which is called 'Eddie's Brother.' The episode should be shown sometime in February.

Immediately prior to that, he spent two weeks working on a pilot for Universal Pictures called "Stranded," which starred Richard Egan and Fernando Lamas.

And just before that there were roles in "Gomer Pyle," "Jesse James", "Bewitched", "Please Don't Eat Th Daisies", "Bonanza", "Th Virginian" and others. I seems he handles comedy an drama with equal dexterity.

A couple of years ago he was filming "The Birds" for Alfred Hitchcock. The famed director was explaining his scene to Rory. "In this sequence, of all the birds flying around, only seven are trained to attack the people. Now you understand about the other birds, don't you?"

"Sure," replied Rory, "they're just extras."

Only a child reared in show business would probably have answered like that and as Rory puts it when asked, "You know, I've been in this business a long time." He has. Since he was 5.

Last season Rory was playing a lead in "My Favorite Martian" and of course, when he works, the studio provides a school teacher on the lot so no school work will be missed.

"Who is the President of the United States," the tutor asked.

Rory's prompt reply was "Lyndon Bing Johnson." Mr. Crosby would probably have been pleased to learn this.

But Rory, despite his acting chores, maintains a straight A average in school. His classmates see him frequently on TV but modest, he finds his fame embarrassing and when they come to congratulate him, he hides in the boys' room to avoid them.

Ash blonde and small for his age , a mere 53 inches, Rory is nevertheless a fine athlete, playing in tennis competition a fine swimmer and horseman. In his young years, he has already achieved over 100 acting

The best kind of call, called 'special requests', meant you were asked for specifically by name and there was only going to be a small handful of people reading for the part. These interviews, or after school appointments as we sometimes called them, included anything from meet and greets just for the casting people or their directors to get a feel for who you were, to script readings, acting out a scene, photo shoots, acting lessons, voice lessons, make-up, wardrobe fittings, meetings with the other cast members to see how your characters melded together, and even meetings with the directors or producers. One such time, I had a meeting with a director who wanted to meet at the commissary lot. He said the bill was on his tab and that I could order anything I wanted. I couldn't believe my good fortune and all I could say was "REALLY?" I ordered a chocolate shake (something I loved but was not allowed to have at home). Mom could not say anything (I watched her fuming from the next table over), as she was desperate to have the meeting go smoothly and I was momentarily free to enjoy my chocolate shake.

THE Hollywood REPORTER — Monday, March 27, 1961

ON THE AIR

With HANK GRANT

[illegible] . . . They cut off his unemployment insurance because "Rory Stevens is no longer eligible for payments due to the fact that he left his [illegible] to get married!" . . . So mama Stevens marched [illegible] and Rory down to the Cal Employment office in Van Nuys on Friday, where they wouldn't give him his insurance till he'd signed an affidavit declaring he is NOT married—in the presence of an attorney! . . . Talking horse "Mister Ed" gets a love interest in the series [illegible]

LOS ANGELES MIRROR 4* — Mon., Mar. 27, 1961—Part I 5

RORY STEVENS helps in "Bringing Up Buddy" on Channel 2 tonight.

RORY STEVENS in "BRINGING UP BUDDY" Tonite—8:30 P.M.—Ch. 2

[illegible]

Rep: Sandy [illegible] Agency

Married? Ha! Rory Doesn't Even Like Girls!

Rory Stevens wants it to be known he's not married.

What's more, he doesn't even like girls!

He made these pronouncements Friday at the Van Nuys branch of the State Department of Employment.

Rory, a television actor, is 6½.

He's been out of work lately—and since his earnings exceeded $6000 in 1960 he's eligible for unemployment insurance benefits.

Accompanied by his mother, Mrs. Elaine Stevens, he went to the branch last Friday to collect his $[illegible] weekly check.

Sorry, he was told, the payments had to be stopped.

Seems that the department had made inquiries to his last employer.

The firm replied he had left in order to get married.

It was an obvious clerical error—but it took a week to be straightened out.

When Rory reappeared at the office now, he promptly got the check.

And he's still looking for work.

—Los Angeles Examiner photo.

RORY STEVENS FIGURES THE FIGURES
This trip the young actor picked up his check.

Pilot TV Series (One of Many)

Back at Home

Home life away from the set was always interesting. As I touched on previously, all four of us kids had a list of chores to complete around the house and yard each week; things like mowing, trimming the bushes, weeding, cutting the ivy back, raking leaves, or picking up the apricots from our trees (when in season), or whatever else needed doing. One day, when Mom and Dad were out running errands, they left instructions for us to remove the weeds growing in cracks in the cement along the patio out back. This seemed like a hard job at the time and I came up with a brilliant idea! Instead of using shovels I decided that we should get some gasoline from the lawn mower, pour it on the weeds, and burn them. So, we set out to find the gas can and poured gas up and down the patio where the weeds were. Then I lit it with a match. The flames immediately jumped up higher than our heads and just a few feet from the house. Stacey screamed, "Call the fire department!" "No," I yelled back, "if we call them Mom and Dad will find out what happened!" It's not like the house was burning, hopefully they would never know. Luckily for us, after a few minutes the gasoline burned off and left the house completely unfazed and waiting for us to explain.

Freezer "Red Alert"

I may have mentioned previously that we had a large freezer in our garage. It was mostly for frozen meats, but Mom liked to buy herself a large carton of ice cream and kept it away from the four of us by "hiding" it in the garage freezer. Eventually, it became clear that she had to do more to secure her hidden treat from us… so she looped a metal chain around the freezer and put a lock on it. Not to be deterred, we tried the lock and chain to find there was enough slack in the chain to carefully reach in with one arm and scoop a bit of the delicious ice cream out with our fingers. Mom could never figure out why her ice cream always had small finger scoop marks in it when the freezer lock was clearly secured in place. We eventually grew bolder and started using a spoon to get bigger bites. However, we could only do this when Mom was off playing tennis or running errands. Since the freezer was in the garage where Mom would drive into when she got home, we had to devise a clever plan not to get caught. We would take turns being lookout – one of us would stand out on the street by the driveway and watch for Mom to come home. When Mom turned up the driveway, we would yell at the last minute "RED ALERT!!!" Once we heard that, we would jump out at the last second. We had no clue what we should do with the spoons so we just started throwing the spoons behind the freezer as Mom pulled the car into the garage. We would never admit knowing how or why the ice cream's level changed as Mom ate it over time… or why utensils in the house kept disappearing. It was rather amusing when we finally sold the house and the freezer was moved… and questions were asked. Why were there so many spoons behind the freezer?

Trampoline Stories

We grew up with a trampoline in the yard (one of the few things we had to entertain ourselves with). In those days there were no safety pads on the metal rails or netting around the perimeter and the trampoline stood about three feet above the ground. Stacey and I loved taking turns doing a combination of seat, knee, stomach, (and the hardest) back drop. I recall one session, on my turn I tried the back drop and came up short, landing on my heels which shot me backwards. My head landed square on the metal bar and then hit the ground. As I lay there trying to collect myself, Stacey called down "why won't you come up and finish the game?" Finally I stood up with my fingers crossed tightly on top of my head. She looked confused and I opened my hands to reveal two bright red bloodied hands. "Mom!" Stacey cried, "Mom, come fast! Mom!!" It took some time before Mom finally came out to see what we were up to. Upon assessing the situation, she turned back towards the house saying it was her turn to rest so she was going to get our father. I still remember Dad collecting me and putting me in the car to head to the hospital… where I collected a nice new row of stitches.

We all loved that trampoline as it was something that filled our days with joy, exercise, games, and play. Our favorite game was called "add a trick." This is where each player had to attempt the tricks given by the previous players and then add a trick of their own for the next player to attempt. As the tricks piled up it became just as hard to remember the order as it was to do the actual series of tricks. For example, one series of tricks might be: knee drop, then knee and a front flip, then knee-flip, bounce to feet, then knee-flip-feet-360 twist, then knee-flip-feet-360 twist, and a stomach drop, then knee-flip-feet-360-twist-stomach-180 stomach twist… and so on down the line until someone missed and could go no longer.

Since our little home had no air conditioning, during the hot Southern California San Fernando Valley nights of summertime, we were allowed to choose to sleep either in our shared bedroom, or go outside and sleep on the trampoline. We loved the cool night air but had to fend off an endless amount of mosquitoes. We usually spent several hours trying to sleep, waiting for the air to cool, before giving up and going back inside to try and get some sleep in our room. When wintertime came we had one old fashioned floor furnace (in the main room) that the four of us would huddle around and fight for space to feel the warm air coming up from below.

After enough time and healing had gone by from the bloody head injury incident with Stacey, Randie had some new trampoline tricks she wanted to try out with me. She double bounced me as high as she could manage and I came down head first (again) landing between the springs.

The next time Randie wanted to try this same trick, she added her best friend Nancy to the act. This time, we had 3 people on the trampoline, two to double bounce, plus me to see how high I could go. There was only one "must follow" rule my parents had for the trampoline which was: **only one person at a time on the trampoline.** So anyhow, Nancy was on the trampoline while Randie climbed up onto the roof. In planned coordination, Randie jumped off of the roof onto the trampoline. This shot me up so high that I could see over the roof tops of the houses and then I somehow turned sideways and shot thru the adjacent glass window that led into the garage and into a sink where I broke my arm… at the exact same moment that Mom was pulling into the garage and Marc was yelling "RED ALERT!!! RED ALERT!!!" Needless to say, Mom and Dad were none too happy with us and forbade us from using the trampoline for a long time after that.

Apricot Trees

(and plum tree)

We had seven large apricot trees on our lot which produced (what seemed like) endless amounts of fruit during the summer growing season. Under Dad's direction, he would climb the trees to pick the ripening fruit, and we were to gather the fruit he dropped onto the ground into boxes. We would bring all of the fruit to the garage sink for washing then split them all open to remove the pit in preparation to either dry or can them. This seemed like an endless job as the sink was repeatedly filled to the top with the endless boxes of fruit. We were taught how to can and put away apricots for the winter, and how to dry the fruit by opening it and laying it on wooden drying racks. We would take full crates of the fruit to all the neighbors as well (I ate so many apricots over the years that I can just think about the taste and it will come to me without needing to see a fruit). One year, Dad had us stack the drying racks one on top of another, then cover them with a very large cardboard box. We lit a small sulfur candle and placed it inside the cardboard box, the sulfur treatment was supposed to keep the fruit a nice orange color. Afterwards we all went off to sleep, tired from a hard day's work. During the night we were abruptly awakened by the sounds of sirens and yelling. The wooden trellis under where the fruit had been laid to dry was on fire from the sulfur candle and the day's work was a total loss.

Plum trees and one across street too!

In addition to the apricot trees, there were also a few amazingly productive Santa Rosa plum trees. When the plum tree was in season (also during the summer time) it blanketed the ground with rich sweet deep purple fruit. On any summer day during, we could be found in the back yard under the plum tree munching away on these precious natural treats.

Swimming Stories

I was not the only one that met the "parent machine"…

Randie, in addition to her other talents, was a terrific swimmer. She worked out at Al Hienrich's Encino Swim night and day preparing herself to be an Olympic-quality swimmer. Mom took pages and pages of notes at each practice session that she would go over with Randie afterward to correct her stroke and attempt to help her shave seconds off her times. After getting home late in the evening Mom made Randie stand in front of a full length mirror and practice her strokes, while Mom reviewed her observations and read from her notes. Randie grew to hate the "Mom swim lessons" and being told what to do each moment as she practiced. This led her to decide that maybe swimming was not in her future after all and she slowly drifted away from the pool and found herself on the volleyball court.

Stacey by the pool, where she was for many, many hours every day

Stacey was also a terrific swimmer (*still is to this day*). Mom took her swimming early every morning before school and then again after school. Just as she did with Randie, Mom took copious notes to go over with Stacey after she was done with workout or practice. During practice, she would run up and down the deck yelling instructions as Stacey swam. Mom even went so far as to attach rubber pulleys to our patio at home for Stacey to practice her strokes between swimming lessons. Mom became so aggressive during practice and at meets she was finally told by the swim coach that if she was going to be there she had to stand behind the fence and mind herself. She would not be deterred, however. She would make signs with instructions on them and held them up over her head for Stacey to see as she swam.

Mom and Stacey at a Swim Meet

I was often dragged along with Mom and Stacey to practice, so I would also swim in the pool while they were busy. I would usually end up swimming 20 laps or so and playing on the diving boards. I loved the diving boards. I was told I could play on the low 3-meter board and spent a lot of time there. After I gained enough confidence I knew I could jump from the high dive platform. One afternoon, when no one was paying attention, I climbed slowly and carefully all the way to the final step when I heard a loud yell from Mom, something like "what are you doing up there! Turn around and come down this minute!" I was so rattled by Mom's screams that I turned, slipped, and fell from the top step of the high dive platform onto the concrete deck below. I remember having a lump on my forehead the size of a baseball and a concussion for many years after "the great diving board incident." We always debated whose fault the fall was, but I was convinced that I was doing just fine before Mom started screaming. However you look at it I deemed I was lucky to be alive.

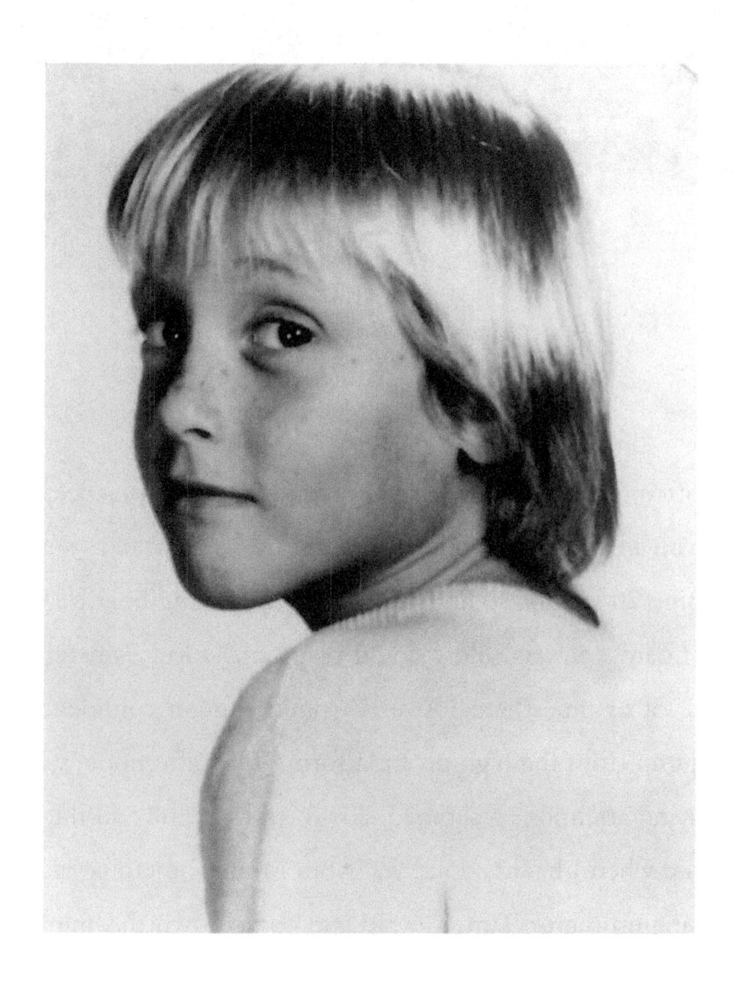

Grandma's Cookies

We often got to go to Grandma Rose's house… which we loved. She always bought us a package of raisin "cookies" to eat. Mom made it clear to us that we were not to eat these but only the healthy foods grandma prepared. So at night, after everybody went to bed, we would sneak into the kitchen to find this sweet treat, and we would eat the entire package of cookies. The next day grandma would ask us where the cookies went. We would claim we had no idea what she was talking about. She would tell us that she bought them just for us, and it was fine for us to have them. However, we were so scared to have Mom find out that we ate a package of cookies, that we would just lie our asses off, even though everyone knew the truth about where the cookies went.

The raisin "biscuits" that we thought were delicious "cookies"!

The Beatings

The beatings became a regular event at our home. If Mom thought we were disobeying her in some fashion, any fashion, out would come the belt and the threats to hit us good with the strap! Mom would use whatever she could grab from the house if the belt was not to be readily found, a stick or a wire hanger would suffice instead.

Randie would tell Dad about the beatings, as she wanted to call the police against Mom. When the police did ever show up at the house asking questions, Mom would order Randie to answer the door and tell the police everything was fine. Mom had already made her threat to Randie clear, if she said anything differently to an officer she would beat her "within an inch of her life."

Getting weighed became a daily event for me, as did the beatings. If we weighed more after school than we did in the morning, Mom felt that meant we were cheating by eating food that was not allotted to us and out would come the belt. We came up with all sorts of ideas to help our weight-related cause. We tried putting things like rocks in our pockets or maybe some sand (we got from the park) for the morning weighing so we would be heavier. Then before the afternoon weigh-in we would simply take some sand or rocks out to make it look like we were not gaining any weight. I am not sure how long that lasted or what success we had before we were caught and the beatings took place in earnest.

There were several times I tried to run away from home to stop the beatings, or stop hearing all the yelling, or stop having to go into Hollywood for interviews instead of being allowed to play with my brother, sisters, and friends. I recall one pleasant afternoon we were all playing in the street, Dad came out and said I had to go to town for an interview with a producer he had lined up for me. Dad said I had to go and said there was no choice. Normally Mom was the one that took me on my interviews but in this case the interview had been set up by Dad through one of his contacts and Dad had promised to have me in Hollywood that afternoon. I argued with Dad that I did not want to go but he was unrelenting. Finally, I decided to try and run. Dad chased me into and down the street. I kept out of his reach for some time (one block, two blocks…) until he finally caught me and took me back to the car where he deposited me, and away we went…like it or not! The next few days, friends and neighbors asked me if that was me running away from my Dad as many people has witnessed this. Not only did I find this extremely embarrassing but we never heard from this producer we had gone to see. A total waste of time, I felt.

I also recall one time my Mom got so angry with me (I truly can't even remember why) that she grabbed my arm and squeezed so hard that her nails dug into my skin leaving deep marks. I went to Dad and showed him the grooves in my arm and the deep purple coloring from the bruising caused by the belting along my side and bottom. I told Dad I was tired of the beatings. I wanted him to call the police and have Mom taken away. He begged me to think it over. He said he had spoken to the police and if we called to report the things Mom was doing the only choice they would have would be to come get her and put her in jail. Dad said he just could not stand for that to happen and begged me not to call.

Another vivid incident, as Mom pulled up to the swim center with both Randie and me in the car, Mom was in a foul mood. She began to punch me in the side of my head, over and over, as she yelled at me, "Fatty, Fat-so! YOU are so FAT!!" With each insult I received a blow to my head until blood started to trickle from my ear. Seeing this Randie tried to protect her little brother by insisting Mom stop… she finally grabbed Mom's arm to stop the blows. Mom opened the door and managed to push Randie out of the car and drove away leaving me to fend for myself. Randie would later tell me "that was the saddest day of her life."

My siblings and I all remember one period of time that Mom and Grandma Rose were continually getting into loud shouting matches in the back of the house. When the bedroom door drifted open and the yelling spilled throughout the little house you could clearly hear every word. Mom was insisting that Rose was depressed and needed to go the hospital to have Electro Shock Therapy. Rose was literally screaming "No No No, I don't want to go to that place, I hate the place" begging Mom not to make her go. "I hate it there, it's a bad place." It was so painful and she was scared and did not want to go. With Rose crying and insisting not to make her go and with Mom getting louder and more demanding, this was a difficult time for us all. After their fights, I would ask Mom why she was making Grandma Rose go when she did not want to go and besides Grandma seemed perfectly fine to all of us. Mom insisted that Rose was depressed and this was the only way to help make her better. Mom would not back down and eventually got her way. I do not truly recall what happened to Grandma Rose other than the fact that we saw much less of her after her time at the hospital. My sister Randie remembers Grandma Rose afterwards and says she basically came back after several "treatments" and no longer spoke. She never smiled after that or interacted with us. She mainly just sat quietly by herself on the couch looking depressed. Randie has a photo of her like that sitting on Steve's parents couch during her wedding. So sad.

One day, I decided to walk away and just keep walking wherever that took me. I did not care. I just wanted to be away from all the noise and violence. So I walked through Van Nuys, through Panorama City, I went and just kept walking. I never knew the peace and quiet I felt. Into the foothills I went until finally there no more houses or streets, the ground became soft and lined with tall trees. With no place left to walk, I sat down, eventually fell asleep, and woke and listened as the night grew dark around me. Overcome with all the quiet around me I did not know where to go or who to talk to, so after some time I finally stood and started walking back from the direction I came. Back into the neighborhoods I had passed earlier. I walked for hours and hours. When I saw someone look at me, I walked purposely faster with strong confidence in my step. I put on a mask of "this is where I belong, and don't mess with me" as I walked. With this real acting persona on, I went back through Panorama City, and then later back through Van Nuys, and then after a full day and evening of being gone from the house, I came to my neighborhood and turned down my street only to see many police cars in our driveway and on our street. My parents had called the police as I was "lost" and could not be found. As I walked up my drive, one policeman yelled, "Here he is, I think we found him on the driveway." I didn't know what type of beating I was in for that night as I was tired and simply didn't have the energy to care. Thankfully, that beating never came to pass… the family and home were all quiet for the night.

Acting Parts: Ages 10-14

1964 – 1968

Junior High School

The acting roles continued coming in and were doing fine… however, life at home just kept getting weirder.

At home, and now in Junior High School, I badly wanted to have a few coins to buy myself a snack at recess, especially when the cafeteria made mouth-wateringly-delicious sourdough bread rolls with melted butter. I did not have any money for snacks (or anything else for that matter) and when the bell rang for classes to start and the other kids left their half-eaten snacks on their trays and ran to class, I helped myself to their delicious treats! Happily eating the morsels left behind by my classmates.

Movies ★ Drama

By HAZEL FLYNN

The Beverly Hills Citizen Mon., Mar.

Rory is New Rave But Shucks He's Only Six

Rory Stevens, handsome blonde actor (now don't get excited girls, he's only six years old), who played a role in Playhouse 90's "Sound of Trumpets" recently, and has been chosen for an important part in "Brotherhood of Evil" a scheduled feature film, is a young man of many talents.

Professionally, he started out as a model at the age of two and a half, and has a multitude of top modeling jobs to his credit. He was also selected as "Mr. Wading Pool" of 1957 in a city wide contest.

Represented by the Comorra-Bernbrock Agency, he has worked on the "Roy Rogers TV Show", Captain Grief TV film "Escape", the "Playhouse of Stars" and done TV commercials.

Rory's private life is most interesting of all. Not only does he have an extremely high I.Q. and can read, write, tell time and do arithmetic problems, but he is an all around athlete. A champion swimmer, he is excellent on skates and horseback riding.

Rory is enormously self-sufficient, well beyond his years and has tremendous stick-to-itiveness. Becoming absorbed in any project, he will work at it until his task is completed. He sketches and paints. He is a very level-headed chil*.

Shy and soft-spoken on interviews, he nevertheless has an adorable personality which wins friends and influences people wherever he goes.

RORY — Rory Stevens, child acting find, has im-

It was always about food… I told my Dad in the evenings about how I was able to eat at lunch but was never able to buy any of the food myself. At some point I noticed that Dad always left a few coins in his pants pocket when he hung them up for the night before bed. I had the very brave idea, when I dressed for school one morning (and Dad was still asleep) that I would sneak into his room (ever so quietly) and look in his pants pocket hoping to find some coins. I would take a few coins (enough for a slice of bread) and leave the rest so he would not notice. One day, when we were a bit older and the topic came up, Dad told me "those coins were put there for you to buy your buttered bread. I was so happy each morning to pretend to sleep while I watched you come in and take the coins you needed to eat."

At home in the kitchen helping Mom to prepare the evening meal, my sister Stacey and I noticed some dog kibble spilling out of the refrigerator onto the floor. We both looked close to examine what this was. We quietly debated if it was safe to eat and quickly agreed that if it did not hurt the dog, it should be safe for us. We secretly put it in our pockets or into our mouth when Mom was not looking. We decided it was fine and enjoyed the dog food as a nice snack. Not long after, I got called to go on an interview for this same brand of dog food that I had eaten off the floor. I got the job because I told the producer that I thought the dog food was great! Little did he know I spoke from personal experience.

Things with food continued to reach new heights as Mom found ways to tie up all the food (literally) in the house so she would know if anyone had touched it, much less eaten any of it, without her permission. This became a huge problem in our family of growing teenagers. We were hungry all the time. First, she would label all the foods in the fridge with notes like "food for Randie and Marc", or "food for Stacey or Rory." Most importantly she would label some food items with "FOOD FOR MOM ONLY", (or) "FOR ME ONLY", (or) "DON'T TOUCH THIS PACKAGE", (or) "HANDS OFF THIS ONE", (or) "LAST ONE FOR MOM ONLY!" There was Hell to pay if anyone disobeyed the notes and signs that were literally everywhere.

Mom started tying all the cabinets (that had food inside) closed with shoe laces. She said she could tell if anybody untied and opened them. To be certain, she would add a paperclip or a toothpick so if the door was opened the clip or pick would fall and she would know. Mom basically intimidated us to just try and take any food not labeled with your own name! Once we got the cabinet open just enough to squeeze one arm in and secure a bottle of juice. We shared the sweet liquid until it was half way down, then we filled it up to the top with water and put everything back just so. We were hungry all the time.

Into Middle School I went, this was the time when Mom and Dad figured out how I could be eligible for Unemployment Insurance between each of my acting jobs. I remember they filled out forms for me to sign each week and I would have to stand in line with either Mom or Dad to collect the $65.00 per week I was allotted for being "unemployed." I have photos of myself in Mom's or Dad's arms holding up this cash. Where any of this money went, I never knew then, nor ever will now.

TV-RADIO BRIEFS

Shelley Fabares of Screen Gems' "Donna Reed Show" graces the cover of Teen Magazine for June and is top-lined in the lead story about teenagers' behavior.

Singer Jerry Wallace guests on Lloyd Thaxton's "Record Shop" over KCOP-TV tomorrow morning to promote his latest Challenge disc, "You're Singing Our Love Song to Somebody Else."

CBS-TV won two Albert Lasker Medical Journalism Awards, only ones given to broadcast media for 1959, at the 11th annual awards luncheon in NY. "CBS Reports" program "Population Explosion" and the CBS-owned KMOX-TV in St. Louis were the specific recipients.

Ken Murray will appear next Thursday on the Lee Giroux Show over KRCA to discuss his book, "Life on a Pogo Stick."

Moppet Rory Stevens, who appears next in "Wally Goes Into Business," a "Leave It to Beaver" episode, has been set for a front cover of American Weekly.

Siobhan McKenna will co-star with Walter Slezak in "The Woman in White," Dow Hour of Great Mysteries, airing May 23 via NBC-TV.

Clete Roberts' U.S. Television Newsfilm will provide film coverage of May Day celebrations in both East and West Berlin and in Bombay, India, with the footage to be flown here immediately airing. Roberts now is on a worldwide

"Hey Teacher" Pilot with Dwane Hickman

About this time the fighting between Mom and Dad had also reached new heights and they fought almost non-stop. Mom wanted a divorce and Dad simply refused to sign the divorce papers. They finally agreed that Dad would move out of the family home and into an apartment building he was currently managing. We all remember going there on weekends and swimming with Dad as we played our favorite game of whale and minnow. We all begged Dad to move back home. I don't recall how long this went on but I would guess somewhere between one and two years before Mom relented and let Dad return. He agreed to move into the small room addition that had originally built for Randie and Mom would build herself a new bedroom suite in the back of the home.

And that's how we lived going forward.

Kayro Productions

EVUE STUDIOS · UNIVERSAL CITY, CALIFORNIA · TELEPHONE POPLAR 2-2171

January 25, 1961

Elaine Stevens
5529 Sunnyslope Avenue
Van Nuys, California

Dear Mrs. Stevens:

Thank you for sending your suggestion for a series to star Rory. I hope you're successful as you know how much of a Rory fan I am.

My very best.

Sincerely,

Irving Paley

IP:kr

But none-the-less, the acting work continued…

When I was between 10 and 14 years of age, I had parts in popular shows such as The Munsters, Gomer Pyle, Jesse James, Bewitched, Please Don't Eat the Daisies, The Virginian, The Fugitive, and Playhouse 90. Other shows included a lead role in My Favorite Martian, and a lead role in Bringing up Buddy (a new TV Series I was cast in). My work at that time also included a featured role in Daniel Boone and I starred in yet another new comedy pilot called "Hi Teacher" (with Dwayne Hickman). The roles continued to roll in with parts in Murder Me, The Untouchables, a visit to the Red Skelton Show, and a visit to the The Lou Grant Show. I was doing all of this as well as many nationwide commercials at the same time.

Tuesday, October 30, 1962

Hollywood REPORTER

Rory Stevens in Pair

Eight-year-old Rory Stevens has been signed for a featured role in "Flowers For My Love" episode of "The Untouchables" and for a stanza of "Going

Untouchable 'Flowers' For Barbara Stanwyck

Barbara Stanwyck has been signed by Desilu programming veep Jerry Thorpe to star in seg of "The Untouchables" titled "Flowers For My Love," written for her by Herman Groves and Harold

Thursday, December 12, 1963—Van Nuys (Calif.)

APPEAR ON TELEVISION

Actress Shirley Knight and 9-year-old Rory Stevens of Van Nuys will be guest stars on "How Not to Rob a Poorbox" episode of "Arrest and Trial" series on television. Segment will be aired on Sunday, Dec. 22, over ABC-TV.

Some actors that I worked alongside with left life-long lasting impressions on me (some good and some not so good), for example:

My Favorite Martian, 1964, "Nothing But The Truth" *On Amazon Prime*

I worked alongside Ray Walston for a week on an episode of My Favorite Martian. He got a kick out of teasing me by asking me to "please do him a favor." In between shooting scenes he would ask me to go get him a special drink that he really liked which was somewhere in someone's office on the back lot. He said I just needed to ask around when I got there, it should be fine. So, being a naive kid, I wandered around the lot looking for the right building and when I thought I may have found the right place, I would go inside and ask the people working there. They would laugh and tell me that there were no drinks or anything else there for Ray. They explained that Ray just liked to tease the new actors on the show by sending them on wild goose chases. When I returned to the set, the director was upset with me for not being available when he needed me. I can't say Ray Walston endeared himself to me by these shenanigans as I was just a ten year old kid.

The part I played on the show was a brow-beaten boy of a couple that did not believe in their son (me) having an imagination. So when I told them I had seen a Martian space ship, I simply received a lecture by my Dad that it was not possible as there were no such things. Later in the show when my Dad saw the same space ship he begged me to corroborate his story. I told him what he had made me repeat over and again, "there are no space ships as they do not exist." This part may have been the perfect part for me as I was being brow-beaten by my real parents at home on a regular daily basis. For all I know, this may be what the directors saw in me and may be why they cast me as the right actor for that specific role.

Gomer Pyle USMC with… "Home on the Range", 1965

In this episode, Gomer wanted to find shelter for a homeless family of hillbillies. He succeeded in finding them an old shack not aware that the shack was a target for war games. I had a small part in this episode.

The Fugitive "Approach with Care", 1966

Starring David Janssen as The Fugitive, I was 12 years old and played one of a group of boys playing football until a light haired man ran into our game, knocking down one of our friends and running off with our football. The police arrive and I tell them the man hit and pushed our friend down hurting him. One interesting note about the show was that it was advertised as being "in color" and not in black and white. Color was relatively new at the time.

Bewitched "Junior Executive", 1965 *on Amazon Prime*

Samantha turns Darrin into a 10 or 11 year old kid and my character (at first) bullies him and then becomes his friend as they run and play in the park. Darrin learns, or remembers what it's like, to feel young and free once again. A fun side note about this show is that years later my daughter (born in 1987) saw the tail end of this show and said "Hey, that guy looks familiar!" … and yes, it was me!

My Three Sons "You Saw a What?", 1967 and "Steve and the Computer", 1965

Starring Fred MacMurray. I was 13 years old in the episode, You Saw a What?, but I played a 10 year old boy as I looked very young and was quite small. In this episode, no one believes Ernie when he says he saw a flying saucer. I am one of a group of kids that that makes fun of Ernie for believing he saw this.

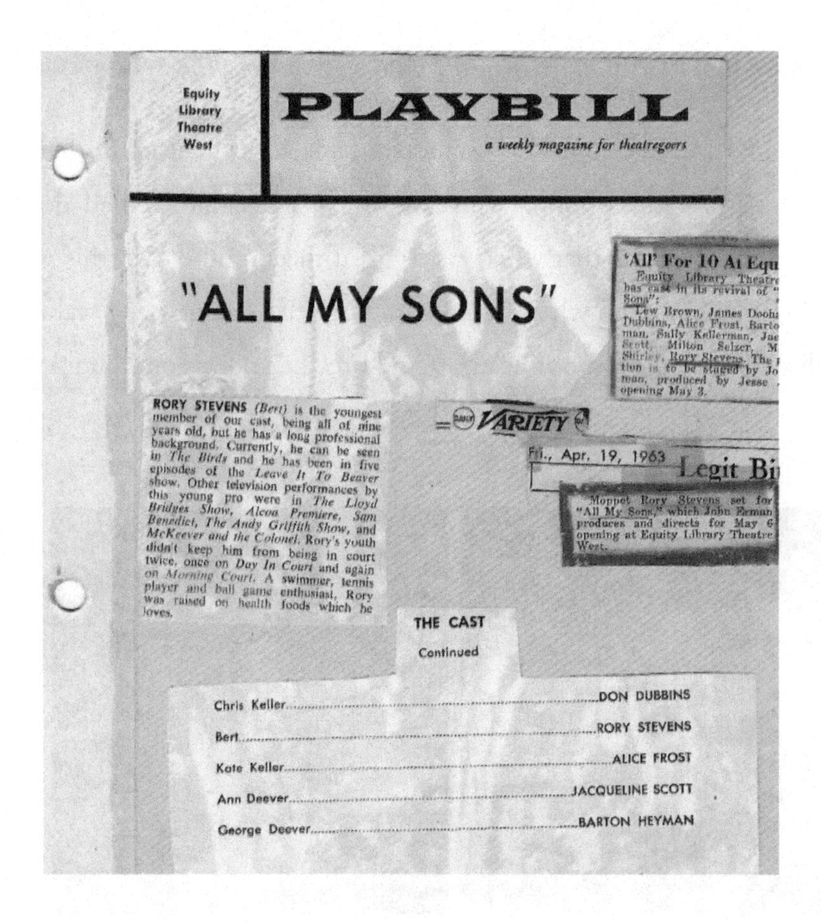

Equity Library Theatre West

PLAYBILL

a weekly magazine for theatregoers

"ALL MY SONS"

'All' For 10 At Equ

Equity Library Theatre has cast in its revival of " Sons":

Lew Brown, James Dooh Dubbins, Alice Frost, Barto man, Sally Kellerman, Jac Scott, Milton Selzer, M Shirley, Rory Stevens. The tion is to be staged by Jo man, produced by Jesse opening May 3.

RORY STEVENS (*Bert*) is the youngest member of our cast, being all of nine years old, but he has a long professional background. Currently, he can be seen in *The Birds* and he has been in five episodes of the *Leave It To Beaver* show. Other television performances by this young pro were in *The Lloyd Bridges Show*, *Alcoa Premiere*, *Sam Benedict*, *The Andy Griffith Show*, and *McKeever and the Colonel*. Rory's youth didn't keep him from being in court twice, once on *Day In Court* and again on *Morning Court*. A swimmer, tennis player and ball game enthusiast, Rory was raised on health foods which he loves.

VARIETY

Fri., Apr. 19, 1963

Legit Bi

Moppet Rory Stevens set for "All My Sons," which John Erman produces and directs for May 6 opening at Equity Library Theatre West.

THE CAST

Continued

Chris Keller.......DON DUBBINS
Bert.......RORY STEVENS
Kate Keller.......ALICE FROST
Ann Deever.......JACQUELINE SCOTT
George Deever.......BARTON HEYMAN

Adam 12 "The Stolen Lawn", 1968 *on Amazon Prime*

Starring Ken McCord and Martin Milner. I was 14 years old now and still playing the part of a 10 year old. I had one scene with Martin Milner where Martin questions me about what I saw when the neighbor had his new lawn stolen, which helped lead to finding the criminals. This was one of the first programs that followed the police as they went through their day.

The Munsters "Eddie's Brother", 1966 *on Amazon Prime*

Eddie wants a baby brother so Grandpa builds a mechanical brother. I play the part of this robot. This was not like anything I had done before and I must say that while it was great meeting the cast, this was not what I had in mind when I considered myself as an actor. I wanted to pull the mechanical robot head off and breathe and act out loud.

Again, I just kept working and working with small parts in:

- Slatterys People (1964)
- Kraft Suspense Theater (Season 2, Episode 29 "Kill me on the 29th", 1965)
- Long Hot Summer (Season 1, Episode 13 "Return of the Quicks", 1965)
- The Virginian (Season 4, Episode 12 "Laramie Road", 1965)
- Please Don't Eat the Daisies (Season 1, Episode 16 "Swing that Indian Club", 1965)
- The Felony Squad (Season 2, Episode 5, "The Death Bag", 1967)
- Pistols and Petticoats (Season 1, Episode 22 "The Golden Fleece" 1967)
- Laredo (Season 2, Episode 1, "Legend of Midas Mante" 1966)
- along with dozens of commercials and seemingly endless interviews, callbacks, and meetings

I was a busy boy.

G.E. Theater Production of Labor of Love

G E Production "Last Day"

I had to be home schooled when I was on the set, as the laws required the studio to provide three hours of schooling per day (with an accredited teacher) if you were working over a certain number of weeks per year, which I was. The teacher had to get my assignments from my regular school so I could keep up with my normal class and she had to keep track of the time clocked in the "school session," as anything less than 15 minutes did not count, so everybody has to be aware of how long you have been "clocked in" before running off to shoot a scene. The other kids at my public school noticed that I was out of school quite a lot; they eventually figured out what I was up to and when I came into the school yard they would often run up to me and say things like, "I saw you on TV last night" and "do you know what you said?"… (well yes I did know what I said)… but they would always choose to repeat my lines over and over again back at me no matter what I said to them. I came to find this very uncomfortable and even downright embarrassing, as I just wanted to be a normal boy with normal friends. Eventually I responded to this attention by never wanting to talk about this aspect of my life with anyone. I was too shy to even watch myself on the TV at home when I knew for sure that something I was in was going to be playing that evening.

McKeever and the Colonel

Acting Parts: Ages 14+

1969 +

As I grew into my teenage years, the acting roles kept me away from the home front… and that was fantastic. I landed small roles in several movies, such as Carrie, Ruby, and How to Murder Your Wife (I continue to get very small residuals for my part in Carrie every year around Halloween and some of the checks are so small they are less than $1.00). Action shows I played parts in included Kraft Suspense Theater, The Long Hot Summer, Laredo, and Adam 12. The comedy roles kept my acting career going strong with recurring roles on One Day at a Time, Room 222, and appearances on The Brady Bunch, My Three Sons, and Bewitched. I also had a few small movie roles in Hollywood High and Malibu Beach. I worked on all of these projects while continuing working on more and more commercials and advertisements.

Long Hot Summer

Crest Toothpaste

One such national commercial was for Crest Toothpaste which brought a lot of attention to me. This was a big deal, a national commercial, and I recall going on multiple interviews and readings for this spot. In the commercial I work at a drug store as a stock boy and there is a bare spot in the shelf (where the Crest is supposed to be). My boss lets me know why it is so important to have the Crest out on the shelf because of what a terrific product it is. At which I respond "Well, I better stock the shelves with some more Crest then!" The interesting things was that when I was in the fourth and final interview doing a reading with all the people involved (the actors, directors, producers, product supervisors) and the actor playing the store owner read his long speech about the product. Right as he finished, it was my turn to speak. I momentarily spaced out for about a single second and 'woke' back up in time to deliver my line in a very enthusiastic manner. The producers and directors all loved it! They told me that they loved the way I paused momentarily to let the information sink in before jumping right into my punch line. I was so happy to get the part so I did not let anyone know exactly what really happened.

TV shows at this time included:

One Day at a Time "Jealousy", 1972 *On Amazon prime*

When I was 18 years old, I landed a very cute scene on a comedy show, One Day At A Time, starring Mackenzie Phillips and Valerie Bertanelli. The episode was called "Jealousy." The scene was with Mackenzie and Valerie and was about me dating Mackenzie. When I came over to her house to pick her up, she was stuffing her bra with tissues to make herself look larger-chested only to hear me tell her Mom that "what I liked about her was how REAL she was." I really enjoyed working with the ladies on that show. They were good, kind, and total professionals that were pleasure to work with (I think they felt good about me too as I was asked back to participate in another episode).

Room 222 "Walt Whitman Goes Bananas", 1972 and "Lift Thrust & Drag"

In 1972 I was also in a few episodes of the TV series, Room 222. "This drama was about life in a multi-racial high school, discussing socially relevant issues of the day, leaving an indelible mark on pop culture." I played one of the high school kids and was glad to be asked back. Even though I was 18 years old (technically still high school age) I looked much younger than my contemporaries… and had shoulder length hair to boot.

Daniel Boone: "Tale of Prater Beasley" *on YouTube*

I landed a guest lead role on an episode of Daniel Boone starring television icon Fess Parker. In the episode my character was crippled. Much to my show father's disappointment, I was constantly coddled by my mother. They fought over how to raise their crippled son. I was berated by my father about how to I should get out and find my way to becoming a man. In the story, I met up with a traveling musician and storyteller who showed me how to find strength from an old Indian legend. With this knowledge and my newfound confidence in myself I ran away from home, only to find my father who was injured and trapped by falling rocks. I helped save his life.

Much of that role had me working with the actor that played Danielle Boone's son (Darby Hinton) as he was one of the stars of that series. He constantly displayed odd behavior, such as being purposefully rude to people that approached us to talk with us. It was not necessary at all and I was confused by his behavior. So at some point I decided to ask him why he acted this way to others. I will always remember his response to me, which was "I like to act this way, it makes me feel good." It was at that moment that I decided that I would never want to behave in such a manner and have always tried to be a kind person towards all people I meet.

RORY STEVENS
Featured Guest Star In
"DANIEL BOONE"
Tonight 7:30 Ch. 4
rep: MARCELLA BELL

Acting Parts: High School & College

As I moved forward into my high school years, several things happened. The most notable was that I was burning out on all of the acting work. To be honest, I had been losing interest for some time and was ready to let go of this part of my life. I will never know for sure but, this may be why I was getting fewer and fewer roles. I started telling Mom that I was thinking about quitting all together. I can't remember ever seeing her angrier than at that moment. She raved and yelled and threatened me. This time it was not with a simple beating but with the threats of psychological warfare. Mom told me that if I wanted to quit, then she might as well burn all of the photo albums she had of my work – photo albums simply filled to the brim with photos of myself with different movie stars, as "I would not be needing them anymore." We "debated" this topic with one other for days and weeks. Her threats were difficult for me to understand as lots of time and energy had gone into my work and I knew that Mom knew those photos truly meant a lot to me, I simply did not wish to continue acting. As I "debated" with Mom about this and thought the decision over, Mom did decide to destroy two of the three photo albums. To this day I am still saddened by their loss. There are so many roles I was in where no photos exist now thanks to her wanton destruction. As you might imagine, the one remaining album I have is a souvenir of great importance to me. My sister Randie recalls that Mom also threw out most of our family picture albums with my acting albums, and Stacey recalls that most of her swim medals and memorabilia were thrown away by Mom as well. It is hard to understand why she would do such hurtful things to her children, but it is sadly all true.

At about the same time, I started asking my Dad where all of the money I had earned acting over the last 15 to 20 years had gone. He never had an answer for me. I always sensed he felt badly and did what he felt that he had to do to keep the family fed and surviving. As I grew older, I figured out that the checks in my name from my acting roles came to our mailbox on a regular basis. I just had to get to the mailbox first in order to claim it. With being away at school and all of my commitments after school, I recall that I was able to grab a check maybe two or three times. The point here is that I was finally starting to challenge my parents for what I felt was rightfully mine.

"Carrie" Movie which still pays (very small) residuals

RORY STEVENS

S.A.G./A.F.T.R.A.

HEIGHT . . . . 6' 2"
HAIR . . . . BLOND
EYES . . . . BROWN

Movies
e.g. "Two For the Seasaw," "The Birds"

75 T.V. leads
e.g. Drama - "The Long Hot Summer"
Comedy - "Dobie Gillis," "Room 222,"
"Adam 12," "My Favorite Martian,"
Western - "Daniel Boone," "Bonanza,"
"Virginian"

Recurring parts in T.V. series
e.g. General Hospital, 4 T.V. Pilots

Stage experience - Legitimate Theatre
e.g. "Equity Library West" – Beverly Hills
"All My Sons"

Voice overs

Skills
Excels in all sports, e.g. surfing, tennis, &
guitar

Interestingly, as I grew into adulthood and started receiving "earnings records" from the Social Security Administration, I learned that my first earnings were prior to the age of six in the amount of $215.00. Each year from then forward, the records show I continued to work and earn a decent income. None of which I ever saw. Many times earnings were in excess of the social security's maximum earnings threshold.

These factors also influenced my decision to call it a day with my acting career and to move on with own life. Mom told me that if I wanted to quit, I would have to call my agent and let her know that I was quitting. This was the last arrow in her quiver. I will always remember the day I called to let my agent know I was done and to stop submitting me for consideration for any further acting jobs. This was the most painful, most difficult decision I had yet made for myself in my young life.

RORY STEVENS

MOVIES

*RUBY
CARRIE
THE BIRDS
HOW TO MURDER YOUR WIFE
*MALIBU BEACH
TWO FOR THE SEESAW
RALLY ROUND THE FLAG
MR. PENNYPACKER

STAGE

ALL MY SONS (EQUITY LIBRARY THEATER)

PILOTS FOR TV SERIES

HOLLYWOOD HIGH
HEY TEACHER with DWAYNE HICKMAN
WHACKY WORLD OF LENNIE WEINRIB
ARREST & TRIAL
STRANDED

DRAMATIC ROLES

DANIEL BOONE (Tale of Prater Beasely)
BONANZA (The Legacy)
WAGON TRAIN (Nancy Palmer Story)
THE VIRGINIAN (Laramie Road)
THE LONG HOT SUMMER
DR. KILDARE
ALCOA PREMIERE
LLOYD BRIDGES SHOW
SAM BENEDICT (7 Gyspies)
UNTOUCHABLES (Flowers for my Lov
G.E. TRUE (The Last Days)

COMEDY ROLES

ONE DAY AT A TIME (Jealousy)
ADAM 12 (Log #101)
THE BRADY BUNCH (Going Steady)
MY THREE SONS (You Saw a What)
" " (Steve and the Computer)
THE MUNSTERS (Eddies Brother)
PLEASE DON'T EAT THE DAISIES
MY FAVORITE MARTIAN (Nothing but the Truth)
McKEEVER AND THE COLONEL (By the Book)
" " " (Blackwells Stand)
LEAVE IT TO BEAVER (Chuckies New Shoes)
GRINDLE (Active Retirement)
BEWITCHED (Junior Executive)
GOING MY WAY (Keep an eye on Santa Claus)
" " (The Shoemakers Child)
BRINGING UP BUDDY (Buddys Wife)
ANDY GRIFFITH SHOW (Andy and Opie, Housekeepers)
JOEY BISHOP SHOW (Every dog should have a boy)
ROOM FOR ONE MORE (THIS GUN FOR SALE)
" " " (a friend in need)
DICK VAN DYKE SHOW (Father of the week)
SHLITZ PLAYHOUSE (The press agent)
GOMER PYLE (Home on the range)

SPECIAL SKILLS

horseback riding
tennis player
swimming
diving
surfing
skateboarding
skiing
trampoline

LIVE TV ROLES

MORNING COURT (the rise and fall of angel face)
DAY IN COURT (the paraplegic plantiff)
GENERAL HOSPITAL (seg. 25,26, 33, 34)
THE JACK BENNY SHOW
THE RED SKELTON SHOW

My Resume of What I was Leaving Behind

When my high school class lined up for our graduation picture, I was literally the smallest boy in the entire graduating class at 5' 7".

My first "real job" after high school was at an Arby's Roast Beef sandwich franchise quick service restaurant. They wanted to pay me the minimum hourly wage of $1.65 per hour, but offered to let me eat all I wanted in return for lowering my hourly wage to $1.35 instead. Little did they know that with some actual regular nourishment, I would quickly grow (practically in one summer) into a 6'4" man. I would arrive at work early for every shift so I could have a decent filling meal before starting work. I would almost always be found holding a chocolate malt in my hand throughout my entire shift. During breaks I would eat again, much to my boss' amazement. Finally, after work while we were cleaning up for the day, I would eat again. I remember saying that my bones hurt from growing so much so quickly. Later I was fired for "eating too much." Unfortunate, but I was so thankful for the time I did have working there (approximately a year and a half) and the fact that it helped me to finally grow to the height I was supposed to be. My parents had managed to keep me looking as small and as young as they possibly could to keep the acting roles coming in so that they could keep their little "money machine" flowing. I was just so hungry… that was all I could really think about.

After I graduated from high school, Randie sold me her car. It was a beat up Ford Valliant with push button controls which she sold it to me for $350.00. The seat coverings were worn away and so I put a folded blanket on the seat to sit on. I was simply so happy to have my first set of wheels and my first true taste of freedom. One year later I managed to buy a Volkswagen Bus for approximately $1,700.00. I paid for it with some of my acting money that I had to beg my Dad for… which he reluctantly agreed to give me. Randie asked me if I would drive her and her new husband Steve around for their honeymoon – which was to be a road trip up to Northern California. I was honored to be asked and off we went on my first real journey out of town.

About this time I was also experimenting with smoking marijuana… which was a pretty popular thing to do at the time. One evening, a group of my high school friends and I had a joint that we suggested sharing outside the house by the curb, so nobody would be able to smell the aroma. As our luck would have it, just as we were inhaling the smoke, my Dad drove up in his convertible and turned right next to us into the driveway. He got out of his car and without stopping or missing a beat said, "Ahhhh, the sweet smell of marijuana in the evening," and kept right on going into the house. Nothing further was ever said on the topic.

Looking back at our family life with the four of us siblings, I think I understand a bit better the dynamics of what we all experienced and how it relates to family "placement" and treatment based on that "placement."

My mother mostly likely did not like men very much, as her life was controlled by men and she felt that she was not allowed to pursue her dreams of going to college or becoming a doctor or a news reporter… simply because she was not a man. Starting from there, and looking at my oldest sister Randie (the first born) who was beautiful, smart, and talented, my Mom projected her hopes and dreams onto Randie for major athletic and overall life achievements, including entry in a beauty contest when Randie was quite young. Randie, however, had other ideas even from an early age. She was simply not that person. She was as different as could be from wanting the attention and glory that my Mom had sought her whole life and now was seeking through Randie.

Then along came Marc, the next child and a boy, about 17 months after Randie was born. Marc was strong willed from the very beginning and a bit of a bully as he grew (he never put up with anything from Mom). The rest of us kids were a bit afraid of Marc (at least to some degree) but we also admired him at the same time since he would stand up to our Mom on our behalf. In later years, Marc would say that he just did not like things that were not fair as he had a strong sense of justice. As adults, we found out that at some point our Dad had asked his family in New York to take Marc to live with them because our Mom felt he was too "difficult." That crossed two kids "off the list" for my Mom to control and mold into what she wanted.

Next came me, a small, pudgy but cute, little boy who was very passive, not very active, but pretty happy with life in general. In other words, someone she could easily control. Someone who would follow her instructions without fighting back and get the acting roles she so desperately wanted her kids to have. Someone she could take out her anger on, anger at her own life not turning out how she wanted it to.

Finally Stacey arrived, who was a lot more like me – passive and just trying to get along in this complicated family; a sweet girl who did her best to avoid conflict and avoid getting "in trouble" with Mom or any of her siblings. Stacey was finally the girl Mom had wanted, a child to "follow in her footsteps" (in her mind) and become all that she had wanted in life for herself.

Thinking about the family dynamics in this way has helped me to understand what happened to me and to all of us kids. I am fortunate to have them as my friends and partners to this day.

The Four Shevin Siblings at Stacey's wedding in 1983

The Penfield House

While in my college years, I told Dad that I wanted to move out of the family home and make a go of it on my own. I was convinced I knew what I needed to do and had the funds to live on my own.

Rent	$
Security Deposit	$
Utilities-Gas	$
Utilities-Water	$
Utilities-Electric	$
Utilities-Trash	$
Insurance	$
Furniture	$
Food	$
Clothing	$
Car	$
Auto Insurance	$
Gas, Repairs	$
Entertainment	$
Sports-Tennis	$
Sports-Surfing	$
Health Insurance	$
School	$
Books	$

Since I was no longer doing any acting, Dad said I would not be able to afford to live on my own. He sat me down, took out a pencil and paper, and made a complete list of the expenses that I would incur. I am telling you that Dad continued on until the paper was full from top to bottom. I was truly flabbergasted at the long list and amount of expenses. I was stunned. I had no clue what it took to have a place of my own. What I did know, unfortunately, was that I had no money at all and could not afford this list of monthly costs. Strangely enough, I was actually earning sizable amounts of money from my television acting roles, movie roles, and commercial spots. I was still receiving residuals and unemployment insurance but I was never taught anything about money, finances, or budgeting.

All this despite "The Jackie Coogan Law" which aims to ensure the financial well-being of child actors by mandating that their employer set aside 15% of the actors gross earnings in a Coogan Trust Account, where it can be monitored –but not withdrawn– by a legal guardian until the child reaches legal maturity.

So Dad made my brother and I a deal. He would buy a house with a guest house and Marc and I could live in the guest house as long as we liked. This sounded good to us and off we went looking at houses that were for sale within a certain price range and within a certain area. On one such outing, we found a house for sale on Penfield in Woodland Hills, California that seemed to match all of our requirements. When we went up to the door to inquire, we were told that the house had just been sold and was no longer available. Dad had a great idea to go ask the next door neighbor if their house might possibly be available for sale as well. I was so embarrassed to go up to the door, as it was clear that this house was not for sale, and I argued unsuccessfully against this. Dad was not bothered at all and actually received a very positive response – the neighbors were indeed interested in selling the property. The property in question also matched all of our requirements, with a main house plus a real pool and a large guest house in the back for us.

Within a few days a deal was struck (much to my amazement) and within a month this was to be our new home. Little did I know the implications of making this sale, as this was the first real estate transaction I had ever been a part of. I had no way of knowing that this was to be the first in a long line of real estate transactions that were to come later in my life.

As we moved in during a chilly winter month, Marc and I quickly discovered that there was no functioning heater in the guest house. We were both too excited to be in our own place that we did not even consider staying in the main house for any length of time. We ended up breaking up all the wooden dressers, furniture, and other wooden items we could get our hands on (like the bed frames) and made ourselves a warm cozy fire by burning all the furniture we had brought to furnish our new home with. While we laughed about this for years to come, we never regretted it for a moment.

Soon after we had all moved into our new home, Dad fell ill and was diagnosed with liver cancer. Within a few short weeks after the diagnosis, he passed away. The doctors told us that he must have been living with liver cancer for at least the last 20 years and no one knew. Mom continued to live in the main house and we boys continued to live in the guest house. By this point in my life both Randie and Stacey had long moved out of the family home and were on their own. My

Dad's death was a pivotal moment in my life, one that I remember vividly, as it happened very suddenly and I found myself adrift without my Dad, who had been the anchor of my incredibly difficult childhood.

The good news is that before Dad passed away he did get his wish as he got to see all four of his children graduate from college and be well on their way to successful careers and lives. He got to see the first blooms of spring in sunny California many times over. He got to own a home of his own with lush grass lawns, fruit trees, and room for a vegetable garden. Most of all, he got to have that family full of kids. All of his childhood dreams had been fulfilled.

Marc and I followed closely in Dad's footsteps. Marc and I both graduated with Bachelor's Degrees from CSUN: Marc with a degree in Philosophy and me with a degree in Geography. We both asked Dad "what should we do now?" Dad suggested that we try working in real estate for the upcoming summer and see if it appealed to us (as Dad was now doing the same thing). For more than forty years after this conversation Marc and I had been working side by side in the field of residential luxury real estate, until my recent retirement, doing just that. We had been one of the most successful teams in the real estate business all these years, working on as little as a handshake and our word. To this day, Marc most closely resembles our Dad, constantly having a quick wit with hilarious jokes and comments about people, their names, and the situations they found themselves in. This is definitely a story for the next saga, coming soon.

Is That Your Mom?

… but back to Mom. At this stage of Mom's life, she took up hobbies to keep herself busy and entertained. She had always been an athlete; in fact she swam daily at the local club up until close to her death. However, as she got older, she had hip issues and other ailments that stopped her from playing tennis and golf, as well as other athletic endeavors of this nature. With those athletic avenues closed to her, she started taking ballroom dancing lessons at the local Arthur Murray dance studio. She started with some free lessons and found that she was quite good and enjoyed dancing a lot. The lessons quickly led to dancing competitions which involved extensive private lessons, dresses, makeup, travel, escorts… you name it. It was a whole deal. In order to win the competitions, Mom insisted she needed to purchase very fancy dresses to compete in, which she did. She also required photographs (which she decorated her house with) and videos (which we were forced to watch), along with the trophies from all of her wins.

The dresses were pure Mom: loud, bright, incredibly gaudy, and padded to give her skinny frame more shape. She was truly in her element with the dance competitions. On any given day, you could see Mom practicing with her "invisible partner" twirling and spinning, either in her home or really anywhere she went. One such time, Mom came with my family to my daughter's horseback riding lessons at the Pony Club in Agoura, California. This is a very dusty and dirty horse environment, but when Mom wanted to do something, there was no stopping her. So here came Mom, dancing away down the middle of the street with her invisible dancing partner. *Is that your Mom? Is that your mother in law? Is that your grandma?*

Another time, she traveled to Yakima where my sister Randie was living and danced and twirled her way through the small local airport where most people knew my sister and her family. "Is that your mother or grandmother?" people would ask.

As you can imagine, all of this was not cheap and at some point we all started to worry that she might run out of money. Mom was also starting to have significant hip issues from the twisting and turning from dancing. So the dancing competitions had to slow down and, surprisingly, once she told her instructors that she had to cut back, they stopped pressuring her to enter every competition. True to form, Mom made the best of the dancing while she was doing it and did it 150%. Probably the same way she did all of the child acting and coaching for us kids when we were young.

At one point, my daughter Amber took dance lessons with her friend Chelsea. This was when she was about 4 or 5 years old. Mom was so excited about this… a granddaughter following in her footsteps! Never mind that Amber was not very good at dancing and just wanted to talk and have fun with her friends at the lessons. We all remember when Mom came to Amber's first dance recital. Mom, with her very skinny frame, was proud of her athletic figure and showed up in, what can only be described, as an "interesting" outfit: black and white Oxford shoes, bright red knee-high socks, a red plaid (extremely short) mini-skirt, a white blouse with red plaid trim, and bright red plaid ribbons in her flaming red hair. It was a sight to behold.

My Mom always wore vivid bright colors to go with her dyed flaming red hair and you could never miss her coming, dancing her twirls and spins down the middle of the street. She looked like she was from another planet. Our embarrassment spilled off our faces as people constantly asked: ***Who IS that? Is that your Mom?***

One time I had a group of friends from my tennis team at Pierce College over visiting at my place. To get into the guest house in the back they had to walk by the glass doors of the main house where Mom lived. As they passed through they saw Mom dressed in one of her wild and colorful outfits simply dancing away, spinning and swooping along the floor only to realize that she was dancing as though she was being led… only she was alone. Of course they all asked: ***Is that someone you know? Is that your Mom?***

I remember one time Mom asked us to take her out for dinner. She wanted to be taken to Wood Ranch BBQ as she had a hankering for a large rib dinner. Mom could put away huge amounts of food even though she was skinny as a rail. True to form, Mom ordered the largest rib dinner they offered. Just after she finished cleaning every last morsel on her plate, she stood up, pulled out a large strand of dental floss, and started working her way around all her teeth in the middle of the restaurant. Not noticing (or perhaps not caring about) the looks of horror on the faces of everyone present in the restaurant as she went. The grandchildren to this day, comment "grandma was always good at flossing everywhere she went." The grandkids (all 12 of them!) seemed to enjoy my Mom's "idiosyncratic tendencies" and often laughed or giggled over the flossing as well as all of the other "interesting" things their grandma did.

My Mom, as a large eater and an older adult, often had gas… which also amused her grandchildren to no end. "How can she not know she is tooting?" they would ask. At one point, the kids had a little machine which would make fart noises and was controlled by a small remote control. They had endless fun placing the machine in grandma's pocket and then proceeded to remotely make the machine do its thing. Mom, at first, tried to ignore it but when that was impossible, would look around in confusion while the grandkids giggled and laughed. In fairness to all of us, they used this machine repeatedly at all family functions, rolling with laughter as it made its rude noises at inappropriate times… so my Mom was not the only victim! As a sign of our total immaturity, my brother took this machine on an airplane flight to Fiji once and used it continuously on the plane as people got up and took things out of the overhead compartments. Yes, we all thought it was hysterical!

Later in Mom's life, when she was no longer able to drive herself around and her eyesight was failing, she started relying on public transportation or family members to help out and drive her around. One such time Mom took the public transit to meet Stacey at a hotel in Westlake Village, California. Mom was waiting by the curb for Stacey to arrive and was (as was now normal at this stage of her life) dressed in old, worn out, baggy clothes… including plastic bags over her shoes to keep them from getting wet. As Stacey pulled up to picked her up, Mom happily commented that the people here in Westlake were "SO NICE" as they offered her food and some even offered her money! Of course Mom never realized that these "nice people" had mistaken her for a homeless person due to her disheveled appearance. However, it was so very obvious to Stacey with one look at Mom's outfit and listening to Mom's story. *OH MY!!!*

As I grew into adulthood, married, and started my own family, my relationship with my Mom remained strained (for obvious reasons). I simply could not get past the memories of my mistreatment as a kid, no matter how happy I was with my current life. Mom was aging now and had many health issues and needs. As such, I simply tried not to get involved with any of them (as I had been inadvertently taught to do as a kid). Her emotional needs, medical issues, or just her desire to spend time together; none of this was of interest to me. My wife Beth was such a trooper and she, along with my sister Stacey, continued to help Mom with all of her appointments until her passing.

They both did their best to protect me from having to deal with Mom, as they knew how upsetting it was for me. However, on one particular day, Mom could not find anyone to take her to a very important doctor visit she had scheduled and with no one left to turn to Mom asked me. I was definitely NOT HAPPY with this but at the same time I could not find it in me to refuse. So off we went, confined in the small space of the car, with nowhere I could hide from her. As the strained conversation bumped along I heard Mom take in a long breath of air and ask what had been on her mind for some time, "Why don't you like me" Mom blurted out. "Why aren't we close," she continued. I looked over at her and the answer was clear, "Because you beat me black and blue almost every day of my life when I was young," I replied. I could then hear her sitting next to me in the car, crying softly. When she could continue she said, "Yes maybe, I was too hard on you." That was the closest I ever got to an apology, or an explanation, or an acknowledgment of how hard and painful my childhood had been thanks to her.

Mom (Grandma Elaine) with a crazy hair style courtesy of her granddaughter

The Legacy/The Family Ranch

Despite our difficult childhood, the four Shevin siblings have remained close throughout life and our children are very close with all of their cousins and (we hope) will remain friends for life too. Our childhood, as troubled as it was, created a sense of closeness among the four of us that we continue to nourish with the values and work ethic that our parents and our grandparents instilled in us. One of our Dad's enduring dreams was to have a "family compound" which he had hoped the Penfield house would accomplish. What he never lived to see was our accomplishment of his "family compound" dream with a land purchase back in the 1980s by three of the siblings, built upon, and enjoyed today by all of the siblings, cousins, extended family, and friends.

The purchased land sat empty for some years but eventually (it took until 2014 before we were able to build and complete the family home) we built a very roomy three bedroom house on the lot – one beautiful bedroom for each of the three families who initially contributed to the purchase of the land. At the time Randie was living in Puerto Rico and then moved to Yakima, Washington; it was simply not practical for her to be a partner in this endeavor, however she and her family stay there while on vacation too and enjoy it and love it along with the rest of us. This "family compound" home is located in gorgeous Santa Barbara County, California and includes an orchard with over 40 fruit trees, multiple large vegetable gardens, and plenty of room for our ever-growing family. We think of Dad every time we pick fruit or see the first flowers of the season on the fruit trees. He would be so proud and so happy to see us all there fulfilling his dream.

We four kids are definitely living our Dad's dream and keeping his legacy alive. This home has been a collaborative effort from start to finish. Everybody has something special included in the home they wanted that would make the dream truly come alive for them. The orchard was the last thing to go in and this was my special "thing" that I wanted. Seeing the blossoms of spring each year along with the salad greens, tomatoes, and peppers always remind me of my Dad. How could it not? We put in an orchard of approximately 40 different kinds of fruit trees, ranging from citrus to stone fruits. This has been great for the lovers of fresh squeezed juices in the family. On any given morning you can see one of us wandering through the fruit trees collecting different kinds of citrus to make a delicious pitcher of fresh juice. These trees, along with the large vegetable gardens, continue to supply an abundance of fresh dinner salads and treats that are a highlight of the property.

This land and this home is our family's meeting place; cousins, aunts and uncles, grandmas and grandpas, Moms and Dads and now grandchildren, (well over 35 people currently) come regularly to join in the fun. Dad told us all about his dream, which was that no matter where in the world you go, there would always be the family ranch to come home to. A warm and loving place that will fill your soul with friends and family, good conversations, and wonderful meals. Dad's legacy is truly alive!

Yes, this story has a happy ending, or at least a happy transition to the next phase in our lives, one which finds the four of us all thriving, happy, healthy, and living a good life, despite, or perhaps because of, our strict and difficult upbringing.

Dad gardening in his plaid pants

Dad with his loud clothes and fruit trees with Marc

Mom – Grandma Elaine

Made in the USA
Las Vegas, NV
06 January 2024